WHY
COLLEGE
MATTERS TO GOD

WHY

AN INTRODUCTION TO THE CHRISTIAN COLLEGE

COLLEGE

MATTERS TO GOD

Revised Edition

Rick Ostrander

Abilene Christian University Press

WHY COLLEGE MATTERS TO GOD
An Introduction to the Christian College
Revised Edition

ACU PRESS

Copyright 2009, 2012 by Rick Ostrander

ISBN 978-0-89112-323-1
LCCN 2009905555

Printed in the United States of America

Scripture quotations, unless otherwise noted, are from The Holy Bible, New International Version. Copyright 1984, International Bible Society. Used by permission of Zondervan Publishers.

The photo on page 50 used by permission of Aus 10 Photoartists, ©2008 Matt Feyerabend.

Cover design by Thinkpen Design, Inc.
Interior text design by Sandy Armstrong

For information contact:
Abilene Christian University Press
1626 Campus Court
Abilene, Texas 79601

1-877-816-4455 toll free
www.abilenechristianuniversitypress.com

12 13 14 15 16 17 18 / 7 6 5 4 3 2 1

CONTENTS

PREFACE TO THE SECOND EDITION...7

PREFACE..11

1. INTRODUCTION
   CHRISTIAN WORLDVIEW AND EDUCATION...15

2. WHERE WE CAME FROM
   A HISTORY OF CHRISTIAN COLLEGES IN AMERICA...............................35

3. LIVING LARGELY
   THE DOCTRINE OF CREATION...55

4. NOT THE WAY IT'S SUPPOSED TO BE
   THE DOCTRINE OF THE FALL..69

5. BROADCASTING MOZART
   THE DOCTRINE OF REDEMPTION...87

6. INTEGRATING FAITH AND LEARNING
   A BASIC INTRODUCTION...109

7. AN EDUCATION THAT LASTS
   THINKING CREATIVELY AND GLOBALLY...127

PREFACE TO THE SECOND EDITION

IN the summer of 2009, after writing *Why College Matters to God*, I took a new position as provost of Cornerstone University in Grand Rapids, Michigan. Having just completed a book that places higher education within the framework of a Christian worldview, I found it ironic that I was joining a university whose professors had just published a book entitled *After Worldview: Christian Higher Education in Postmodern Worlds*. The editors of this volume, Cornerstone professors Matt Bonzo and Michael Stevens, had convened a major conference a few years earlier to discuss the weaknesses of the "worldview" concept and to consider other approaches to Christian education.

Fortunately, upon reading the book, I discovered that the title was intended to be more provocative than iconoclastic—that whatever its shortcomings, the concept of "worldview," properly understood and nuanced, is still an important and useful organizing tool within which to frame Christian education. As one of the conference's more prominent speakers, Albert Wolters, remarked, "If we believe that Christianity teaches the truth about reality and human life, and if we want to communicate to the world around us that this truth is public truth, with implications for the way that human society and civilization ought to be organized and shaped, what other word shall we give to our understanding of that truth?" While not perfect, "worldview" is still the best term available for Christian colleges today.

Moreover, I was heartened to discover that the overall conversation of the conference itself paralleled my own developing thoughts on the subject of Christian worldview and education which are reflected in the second edition of this book. For one thing, I emphasize even more strongly the notion that worldviews are experiential and open-ended, not formalized, air-tight philosophies of life. That understanding is reflected in my crossword-puzzle analogy, which I still believe is an effective and useful metaphor for worldviews even though few students do crosswords anymore. Second, I continue to grow in my appreciation of the fact that Christianity is ultimately a way of life, not simply a set of ideas, and so an emphasis on the "praxis" element in worldviews appears more strongly in the second edition.

The notion of worldview as a lived reality means that Christian educators are concerned ultimately about what our graduates will actually do in the world when they leave our campuses. My thinking on the Christian's relation to culture has continued to evolve since I wrote the first edition of *Why College Matters to God*. Furthermore, it has been shaped by the ongoing conversation (and, at times, debate) among Christian thinkers such as Charles Colson, Andy Crouch, James Davison Hunter, Gabe Lyons, and James K. A. Smith, to name a few, on the question of what we actually want our college graduates to do in the world. The question that Francis Schaeffer asked decades ago—"How shall we then live?"—continues to reverberate across the American Christian landscape, and the ongoing attempt by contemporary evangelicals to answer that question is reflected in the pages of this book, most notably in the chapter on "Redemption."

Overall, I have been pleased with the reception of *Why College Matters to God* in its first two years. In general, it seems to have accomplished its modest goal of communicating the basics of Christian higher education in a brief, understandable, and readable format. Thus, while I have revised the text in light of the ongoing conversations about worldview and culture, I have resisted the temptation to expand the book's scope to incorporate additional dimensions of Christian colleges. For example, the subject of spiritual formation and faith development on college campuses is a vibrant and dynamic topic of study. Rather than expanding my book to encompass the various dimensions of this topic and its implications for Christian education, however, I have kept my primary focus on what Christianity means for academic life, and in particular the college classroom. I hope my book is brief enough to pair with others on related topics, if college leaders believe that additional texts are beneficial for their students.

Finally, I would like to thank the members of my new learning community at Cornerstone University for the counsel, friendship, and—to use a favorite term on campus—"hospitality" shown to my family and me. In particular, the members of the Civitas faculty book discussion group, led sometimes coherently by Matt Bonzo and Michael Stevens, have challenged and influenced my thinking on Christian education. Also, President Joseph Stowell has been a tremendous encouragement and support as I learn the ropes as a chief academic officer. Furthermore, living in the evangelical Mecca of Grand Rapids has been a wonderful opportunity to grow in my understanding of Christian education, and it has been a privilege to live down the street from my friend and former mentor, George Marsden.

And as always, my primary gratitude goes to Lonnie, Ryan, Tyler, Rachel, and Anna, who continue to put up with a husband and father who struggles to enjoy a Saturday morning without the computer, but whose greatest satisfaction in life is hanging out with his family and seeing his children develop into mature image-bearers of God.

Grand Rapids, Michigan
August 2011

PREFACE

SOME books are a result of research and study. Others come from life experiences, or solely from the author's imagination. This book has emerged almost completely out of the college classroom. It comes from my attempt to communicate to the Christian college freshman the nature and purpose of Christian higher education.

Given the wealth of books currently available on Christianity and the life of the mind, one may legitimately ask why yet another volume is appearing in print. The answer is simple: As the supervisor of my university's first-year seminar on Christian scholarship, I tried and failed to find a single, concise, readable text that summarizes a philosophy of Christian higher education and explains it on the level of the typical freshman at a Christian college. The closest thing is Arthur Holmes' influential book, *The Idea of a Christian College* (1975), which gave me and many other Christian educators our first exposure to a distinctively Christian understanding of higher education. But students have changed since Holmes' book was written, as has our understanding of Christian scholarship. So having failed to find an appropriate book, I ended up writing my own.

What I have written on the subject, therefore, is hardly original, and readers will quickly notice the numerous books that have shaped my thinking on the topic. These include works by respected writers such as Andy Crouch, Richard Hughes, George Marsden, Cornelius Plantinga, Clifford Williams, and Michael Wittmer—not to mention earlier Christians such as Augustine, John Calvin, John Henry Newman, and C. S. Lewis. My attempt here has not been to say anything particularly new or profound, but simply to summarize and translate the ideas of more sophisticated thinkers into forms and word-pictures that the typical college freshman can easily grasp.

To do so, I have employed a paradigm of Creation-Fall-Redemption that is common among writers from the "Reformed" tradition of Protestant Christianity. One may question, therefore, whether this book represents a Christian philosophy of education or simply a Reformed approach to education. I would respond in two ways. First, the Creation-Fall-Redemption scheme is employed by a variety of Christian writers who are not necessarily in the Reformed orbit, as is demonstrated by two of the best current books out there, Michael Wittmer's *Heaven Is a Place on Earth* (Zondervan, 2004) and Andy Crouch's *Culture Making* (InterVarsity, 2008). Moreover, the Creation-Fall-Redemption paradigm predates the Reformation and can be found in the writings of Church Fathers such as Tertullian. Indeed, one may argue that the scheme simply summarizes the biblical narrative itself, but that is a theological discussion that I would rather not begin here.

Second, I consider myself to be an evangelical Christian, and one of the strengths of evangelicalism is its interdenominational character, and hence its affinity for borrowing from a variety of traditions. If I were writing a book on liturgy, for example, I would borrow heavily from Episcopalian sources. When it comes to philosophy of Christian education, Reformed Christians, from John Calvin's Geneva Academy to the Puritans at colonial Harvard to the Dutch Reformed educators at Calvin College, have done some of Western Christianity's most thorough and rigorous thinking about how our Christian faith informs our approach to education. Thus, I am happy to borrow from their ideas even though my own induction into Christian higher education came through the less intellectual path of Moody Bible Institute, not Grand Rapids or Wheaton.

A word, therefore, as to my intended audience: I hope that this book will be useful to students at Christian colleges across the theological and denominational spectrum. And while I write primarily for students, my secondary audience includes anyone associated with Christian colleges, including students' parents, faculty and staff, and trustees. Readers who want a deeper and more sophisticated treatment of the subject can read books such as Newman's *The Idea of a University* or Marsden's *The Soul of the American University*. Those who prefer a brief and readable introduction to the subject can begin here.

Finally, several people have advised me on this book and informed my thinking on the topic. I have benefitted tremendously from the wisdom of friends and colleagues throughout American higher education. George Marsden, for example, remains a good friend and an example to me of a Christian who loves God with mind and heart. Colleagues at other institutions, in particular Michael Hamilton, Douglas Henry, and Derek Melleby, have helped me with their wisdom and counsel.

Most importantly, I have benefitted from being part of a vibrant community of Christian learners at John Brown University. I am grateful in particular to those who have advised me on the subject or commented on earlier drafts of this text: Jane Beers, Steve Beers, Jay Bruce, Robbie Castleman, Ed Ericson III, Chip Pollard, Trisha Posey, Jake Stratman, and Dave Vila. In particular, my friend David Brisben collaborated with me on earlier drafts of chapter three and appreciates the doctrine of creation more fully than anyone else I know. I will be leaving JBU soon to become Provost at Cornerstone University, and so this book is dedicated to my friends at JBU.

This book is also dedicated to my wife, best friend, and most trusted advisor, Lonnie, who reads and provides the crucial "normalcy check" for every page that I write. And while this book is intended for current college students, it is also written for my children, Ryan, Tyler, Rachel, and Anna, whom I hope will grow up to become image-bearers of God in every aspect of their lives.

Siloam Springs, Arkansas
March, 2009

1 INTRODUCTION

Christian Worldview and Higher Education

ONE of my favorite Far Side comics depicts a herd of cows grazing on a hillside. With a surprised look, one cow says, "Hey, wait a minute! We've been eating grass!" Like most Far Sides, the comic works because it uses animals to depict a universal truth: In society we often do things automatically without ever asking the question "Why?"

Take college, for example. A Tibetan herdsman visiting America would notice a strange phenomenon. Among the middle and upper classes of society, young people around the age of eighteen complete a certain level of schooling known as "high school." Then millions of them pack up their belongings and move to a residential campus to live with other young people, most of whom they have never met. For the next four or five years, they complete an assortment of classes that collectively comprise what is called "undergraduate education."

Just what are these classes? First, they take "general education" or "core curriculum"—classes such as English literature, history, natural and social sciences, and philosophy—the kind of stuff that people have been studying for centuries. Along with the core, students take classes in what they call a "major" area of study: a subject that they are most interested in or one that they (or their parents) believe will yield the best career prospects. Amid all of this course-work, the students find ample time for eating, socializing, compet-ing in athletics, and playing Halo in the dormitory.

It all may seem quite normal to those of us who have gone through or are going through the process. But our Tibetan herdsman probably would be hard pressed to see the purpose in all of it. His perplexity would increase if he visited a private Christian college, where chances are students pay more money for a narrower range of academic programs and more restrictions on their social lives.

Of course, there are a variety of reasons why students choose to attend a Christian college. For many of them, it's the perception of a safe environment. For others, it's a particular major that the school offers; or perhaps the Christian emphasis in the dormitories, chapel, and student organizations; or the school's reputation for academic rigor and personal attention from Christian professors. It may even be the likelihood of finding a Christian spouse at a religious college.

None of these features, however, is unique to a Christian col-lege. For example, if it's safety you're looking for, you could just as well attend a secular college in Maine, which boasts the nation's lowest crime rate. Moreover, most state universities have thriving Christian organizations on campus that provide opportunities for fellowship and ministry—and more non-Christians to evangelize as well. One can also find good Christian professors at just about any secular university. One of the most outspoken evangelical profes-sors that I had as a college student, for example, was my astronomy professor at the University of Michigan.

The real uniqueness of a Christian college lies elsewhere. Simply stated, the difference between a Christian university and other institutions of higher education is this: A Christian college weaves a Christian worldview into the entire fabric of the institution, including academic life. It is designed to educate you as a whole person and help you live every part of your life purposefully and effectively as a follower of Christ. Such a statement will take a while to unpack in all of its complexity; and that is the purpose of this book. If properly understood, however, this concept will enable you to thrive at a Christian college and to understand the purpose of each class you take, from English literature to organic chemistry. But first we must establish four foundational concepts, the first of which is the notion of worldview.

> *The difference between a Christian university and other institutions of higher education is this: A Christian college weaves a Christian worldview into the entire fabric of the institution, including academic life.*

1. What is a worldview?

About a decade ago, the film The Matrix enjoyed popularity among youth pastors and those who like using movies to discuss deep ideas. That's because amid the fight scenes and big explosions, *The Matrix* forces us to ponder the age-old philosophical question posed by Rene Descartes back in the 1600s: How can I know what is really real? The film begins with the protagonist, Neo, as a normal New York City resident. But gradually he becomes enlightened to the true state of reality—that computers have taken over the world and are using humans as power supplies, all the while downloading sensory perceptions into their minds to make them think they are living normal modern lives. Neo achieves "salvation" when he accurately perceives the bad guys not as real people but as merely computer-generated programs.

The Matrix thus challenges us to recognize that some of our foundational assumptions about reality—that other people exist, that this laptop I'm writing on is really here—are just that: *assumptions* that serve as starting points for how we perceive our world. If my friend chooses to believe that I am a computer program designed to deceive him, it's unlikely that I will be able to produce evidence that will convince him otherwise. Furthermore, as Neo's experience in the film indicates, shifting from one perception of reality to another can be a rather jarring, painful process.

In other words, *The Matrix* illustrates the notion of "worldview"—that our prior assumptions about reality shape how we perceive the world around us. A worldview can be defined as a framework of ideas, values, and beliefs about the basic makeup of the world. It is revealed in how we answer basic questions of life such as, Who am I? Does God exist? Is there a purpose to the universe? Are moral values absolute or relative? What is reality? How should I live my life?

We can think of a worldview as a pair of glasses through which we view our world. We do not so much focus on the lenses; in fact, we often forget they are even there. Rather, we look *through* the lenses to view the rest of the world. Or here's another metaphor: If you have ever done a jigsaw puzzle, you know that the picture on the puzzle box is important. It helps you know where a particular piece fits into the overall puzzle. A worldview does the same. It's the picture on the puzzle box of our lives, helping us to make sense of the thousands of experiences that bombard us every day.

Two important qualifications about this notion of "worldview" are important at the outset. First, a worldview is not the same thing as a "life philosophy." A philosophy of life implies a rational, deliberately-constructed, formal system of thought that one applies to one's world. But worldviews go deeper than that. A worldview is *pre-rational* and instinctive. It is shaped by my experiences and the community in which I live more than by logical analysis. One could say that my worldview originates in my *heart* as well as my head. It's the means by which I "know" not only that $2 + 2 = 4$ but that I love my wife, that my redeemer lives, and what the appropriate "social space" is in our culture. As Christians, we should desire to align our worldview with the truth of Scripture and with sound reason (and that's an important purpose of college). But we need to recognize at the outset that a worldview is rooted in who we are at our deepest level, not just our intellect. As C. S. Lewis remarked in *The Magician's Nephew*: "For what you see and hear depends a good deal on where you are standing; it also depends on what sort of person you are."

Second, it's important to note that worldviews are about *actions*, not just beliefs. As one scholar has stated, it is a view *of* the world that governs our behavior *in* the world. To return to the example of Neo in *The Matrix*: His new understanding of the nature of reality results in a fundamental change in how he lives his life. Indeed, one could say that the actions and practices that order our lives reveal what our actual worldview is, regardless of how we might describe that worldview on paper. In other words, a worldview is a way of life, not just a set of ideas.

We cannot help but have a worldview; like the pair of spectacles perched on my nose, my worldview exists and is constantly interpreting reality for me and guiding my actions, whether I notice it or not. Neo begins *The Matrix* with a worldview; it just happens to be an incorrect one, and he has never bothered to think critically about what his worldview is. One of the main purposes of college, therefore, is to challenge students to examine their worldviews. Which brings me to the next foundational concept.

2. All education comes with a worldview.

Worldviews shape not just our individual lives but universities as well. There was a time when scholars seemingly believed that education was completely objective. Professors in the secular academy, it was claimed, simply "studied the facts" and communicated those facts to their students. Now we know better. All education, whether religious or secular, comes with a built-in point of view. Even in academic disciplines, the worldview of the scholar shapes how the data is interpreted, and even what data is selected in the first place. Nothing illustrates this fact better than the following optical illusion commonly used in psychology:

> *All education, whether religious or secular, comes with a built-in point of view.*

Some viewers immediately see an old lady when they look at this drawing. Others see a young woman. Eventually, just about anyone will be

able to see both (if you cannot, relax and keep looking!). This is because while the actual black and white lines on the page (the "facts,"

so to speak) do not change, our minds arrange and interpret these
lines in different ways to create a coherent whole. Moreover, this is
not something that we consciously decide to do; our minds do this
automatically. We cannot avoid doing so. Neither can those who
visualize the drawing in different ways simply argue objectively
about whose interpretation is the correct one, since their disagreement is not so much over the facts of the drawing but over what
those "facts" mean.

In a more complex way, a similar process occurs whenever
scholars work in their disciplines. Historians, for example, agree on
certain events of the American Revolution—that on April 18, 1775,

Paul Revere rode through the New England countryside shouting "The British are coming!"; that the Continental Congress signed the Declaration of Independence on July 4, 1776; that on December 25, 1776, George Washington and his army crossed the Delaware River and surprised Hessian soldiers at Trenton. But what do these facts *mean*? How are they to be arranged into a coherent whole? When did the American Revolution actually begin? Was it motivated primarily by religious impulses or by Enlightenment philosophy?

Historians argue constantly over such questions, and the answers to them depend in part on the worldview of the historian, who selects and interprets historical data according to certain assumptions about how politics and societies change—ultimately, basic assumptions about what makes humans tick. Thus, a Marxist historian who believes that ultimately human beings are economic creatures motivated by material rewards will likely interpret the American Revolution in a way that emphasizes the financial self-interest of colonial elites. The Christian who believes that human motivation often runs deeper than just economic interests will likely emphasize other factors such as ideas and religious impulses. The "facts" of the Revolution are the same for each historian, but like Neo's perception of his world, the *interpretation* of those facts is influenced by the scholar's worldview.

Or, to cite an example from science: Biologists generally agree about the makeup of the cell, the structure of DNA, and even the commonality of DNA between humans and other life forms. But do such facts demonstrate that human beings evolved from other life forms, or do they indicate that some sort of intelligent being used common material to create humans and other life forms? The answer to this question is not simply a matter of evidence; it is influenced by the scientist's assumptions about ultimate reality.

More generally, not just academic disciplines but entire universities operate according to worldviews. One of the universities that I attended, the University of Michigan, had a worldview that shaped its culture; it was just never stated as such. In fact, one could argue that like many secular universities, my alma mater displayed a multiplicity of worldviews. In the classroom, my courses typically were taught from a perspective known as *scientific materialism*, which could be described like this: the material universe is all that exists; human beings are a complex life form that evolved randomly over the course of millions of years; belief in God is a trait that evolved relatively recently as a way for humans to explain their origins, but now this belief is no longer necessary. Thus, academic inquiry is best conducted when one sets aside any prior faith commitments.

Student life at Michigan, however, typically embodied a different worldview—that of modern *hedonism* or devotion to pleasure. This worldview holds that in the absence of any higher purpose to life, personal pleasure and success are the greatest values. Thus, you should get good grades in college since that is your ticket to a successful career. However, you should not let studies interfere with having a good time, generally defined in terms of parties, socializing, and of course, college football.

Paradoxically, however, a third worldview governed much of campus culture, one best described by the phrase *tolerant moralism*. According to this worldview, intolerance, injustice, and abuse of the environment are the great evils of modern society; racial and cultural diversity and ecological responsibility are the ultimate goods. The actions of individuals and the university community, therefore, are rigorously scrutinized according to how they measure up to these moral values, and anyone from the custodian to the president is liable to censure if their words or actions are seen as detrimental to these causes. A few years ago, for example, the president of Harvard University lost his job because of remarks he made that were deemed critical of women's scientific capabilities.

3. The Christian college: A unified worldview

From a Christian perspective, one could argue that each of these worldviews contains some grains of truth (though we'll wait until chapter three to make that argument). The problem, however, is that the secular university makes no attempt to articulate and apply an overarching worldview that gives a coherent purpose to all of its parts. As a former college president has remarked, the modern university is not a *uni*-versity at all but rather a "*multi*-versity."

> *A Christian university seeks to provide an overarching framework that gives a sense of purpose and unity for everything from English Literature to chapel to intramural soccer.*

A Christian university, by contrast, seeks to provide an overarching framework that gives a sense of purpose and unity for everything from English Literature to chapel to intramural soccer. That umbrella, of course, is a Christian worldview. The novelist Dorothy Sayers once remarked: "We have rather lost sight of the idea that Christianity is supposed to be an interpretation of the universe." The Christian college proceeds from the assumption that this Christian interpretation of the universe, rooted in and supported by Scripture, affects every aspect of the college experience. The particular elements will be explained in greater detail in the chapters that follow. But briefly, the Christian worldview, as described in the Bible, can be summarized as a grand drama in three main acts:

Act 1: Creation. The universe didn't emerge by chance. Rather, an all-knowing, all-powerful, Triune God created everything that exists. Moreover, God called his creation good and delights in it. God culminated his creative work by making humans in his own image and giving them the capacity to delight in creation with him and act as sub-creators in their own right.

Act 2: Fall. Human beings, created with a free will, used their freedom to disobey God. All of creation bears the marks of the Fall, from broken human relationships to tsunamis that wipe out coastal cities.

Act 3: Redemption and Consummation. God, however, immediately set about redeeming his fallen creation and restoring it to its original goodness. The key player in the redemptive drama is Jesus Christ, who came to earth as God incarnate to take the penalty for sin upon himself. Eventually history will culminate in the re-establishment of God's reign throughout the entire universe. In the meantime, the followers of Jesus carry out God's redemptive activity in every corner of creation.

That's the biblical narrative in a nutshell, and it has tremendous implications for a Christian college. Plants thrive when they are exposed to a healthy combination of sunlight and rain. Similarly, we can think of "creation" and "redemption" as complementary purposes that give life to virtually every aspect of a Christian college.

Here's an example in athletics: A Christian college doesn't just have a college basketball team to boost school spirit or attract attention, as secular colleges typically do. Rather, basketball fulfills both a creative and a redemptive purpose for Christians. God delights in his creation, and he created human beings in his image to delight in creation as well. Thus, human play honors God, and developing our ability to shoot a basketball—or spike a volleyball, or swing a golf club—is a way to more fully express God's image.

College sports, however, also bear the marks of the fall. Athletes are placed on pedestals, coaches sometimes cheat, and heated contests can degenerate into hatred toward referees and opposing players. A Christian college, therefore, also plays basketball in order to "redeem" this particular corner of God's creation by fielding teams that demonstrate sportsmanship and fans who display Christian charity to opponents and referees (that's the ideal, at least).

The Christian worldview provides us with a sense of purpose in the classroom as well as on the court. This concept will be explored in detail in subsequent chapters, but for now let me illustrate with an example from a common major, Business. One thing that we learn in the book of Genesis is that God intended for humans to live and function together in community. That's why he created Adam and Eve. He also designed his creation to grow and develop in complexity and interdependence. Today we see that complexity in virtually every aspect of life. Take, for example, my morning cup of coffee, which would be impossible if I were left to my own resources. The beans for my coffee are grown and harvested on a hillside in Colombia. They are transported to my local grocery store, where I buy a half-pound of them for a few dollars. My coffee maker is assembled at a local plant, and the electricity that makes it work is generated by a plant that converts the water flowing from the nearby Grand River into usable power. Simply put, my cup of coffee represents the tip of an iceberg of complex human interactions. And that's a good thing; it's how the world was intended to function.

In its most basic sense, the academic discipline of Business is about learning how to efficiently and justly manage the countless economic and social transactions that we depend on each day; in other words, it's about developing our capacity to live out the notion of human interdependence that was part of God's original design for creation.

The study of Business, however, also has a redemptive component. Unfortunately, economic relations are corrupted by all sorts of individual and structural sin. We see this most obviously, of course, in the corporate scandals that periodically make the headlines. But the effects of the Fall also exist under the radar in economic injustices that might be unwittingly perpetuated even by the coffee beans that I purchase. How does one create a business that pays coffee growers in Colombia a fair price for their beans and still turns a profit in the U.S.? How do communities produce the power needed for their

> *The purpose of a Christian college isn't simply to hand you a complete Christian worldview on a platter; rather, it's to start you on the process of developing a comprehensive, coherent, yet dynamic Christian worldview.*

coffee makers while also caring for the environment? How does one responsibly generate wealth and the opportunity to enable others to benefit from good-paying jobs? These are the sorts of questions that courses in Business must deal with at a Christian college. In other words, Christians don't just study Business in order to make money; they explore how best to practice human interdependence and to redeem economic relations that have been thrown out of whack by the Fall.

In sum, every subject that you study at a Christian college—and everything else you do, for that matter—has a purpose and value within a Christian worldview framework. Discovering what that purpose is, however, isn't always easy, since as the final section explains, worldviews don't stay the same.

4. Worldviews are communal and open-ended.

Our worldview is continually subject to growth and revision as we encounter new people, ideas, and experiences. Thus, the purpose of a Christian college isn't simply to hand you a complete Christian worldview on a platter. Rather, it's to start you on the *process* of developing a comprehensive, coherent, yet flexible Christian worldview.

This doesn't mean that we hold our Christian faith as a tentative hypothesis that we're willing to abandon if some new idea comes along. But it does mean that we hold many of our beliefs loosely and that we remain open to adjusting our Christian worldview as we encounter new ideas and experiences in college.

Let me illustrate it this way: I love crossword puzzles. Back in high school, they got me through more than a few dull classes (and probably lowered my GPA as well). More importantly, crossword puzzles help us understand how knowledge and beliefs actually work. The correct answer to a particular crossword clue is often uncertain. Its "truth" must be supported by other clues in the puzzle. The key to solving a crossword puzzle is to build a network of interlocking answers that confirm each other and form a coherent whole. A completed crossword puzzle in which the interlocking answers confirm and support each other, therefore, is constructed painstakingly through a process of trial and error. Moreover, the truth of a particular answer is rarely absolute but merely relative to the other answers in the puzzle. Here's a simple example:

Across
1. A freshwater fish
Down
2. The top of an arc

¹B	²A	S	³S
	P		
²	E		
	X		

If these were the only questions that you had to answer, the solutions might seem simple: "Bass" and "Apex" seem to fit nicely. But let's add two more clues:

Across

1. A freshwater fish
2. Look intently

Down

2. The top of an arc
3. Meat from a pig

The word "peer" seems to work fine for "Look intently." But after trying and failing to think of "meat from a pig" that begins with an "S," you would probably conclude that "PORK" is the only possible answer to 3 Down. But what about "BASS"? You need to go back and erase the word, change it to "CARP," and the puzzle is solved. How do you know your solution is "true"? Because all of the tentative answers fit together and support each other.

¹C	²A	R	³P
	P		O
²P	E	E	R
	X		K

So what does this have to do with a Christian worldview? Plenty. We can think of our assorted beliefs as answers to particular questions or clues, and a worldview as the entire crossword puzzle formed by these interlocking, mutually-supporting beliefs. Experienced puzzlers use pencils to do crosswords since they know that successfully solving the puzzle inevitably involves going back and erasing earlier answers in light of later information. Of course, some answers are so clearly correct that they can be written in pen. If I get this clue, for example: "Former Chicago Bulls great Michael" (six letters), I can confidently write in "JORDAN" in permanent ink. The key is to recognize what answers are certain and which ones are not.

Obviously, some components of our Christian worldview can be written in pen. For example, if we have a five letter box and the clue is "God's written word," we can safely write "BIBLE" in pen. However, it seems to be human nature to use too much pen when formulating their worldview. For example, Christians in the Middle Ages generally believed that the earth was the center of the universe, around which the sun and planets revolved. When Galileo proposed otherwise, he was placed under house arrest. Why? Because the church interpreted verses such as Psalm 104:5 ("He set the earth on its foundations; it can never be moved.") to teach that the earth is fixed at the center of the universe, and the sun and planets revolve around it. Today, of course, we see such an interpretation as a result of mistaken medieval cosmology, not a necessary "fact" of Scripture. Medieval Christians, however, had penned in as an absolute truth the notion that the earth is at the center of creation when they should have used pencil.

Students often arrive at college with much of their worldview written in pen. In fact, many of us come from churches, schools, or families that encourage us to fill in the puzzle with as much pen as possible. To develop a mature Christian worldview, however, you will need to be willing to use more pencil. In fact, one of the purposes of a Christian education is to help you distinguish which parts of your worldview are open to revision and which parts are not.

The crossword puzzle analogy also helps explain why a Christian college emphasizes the notion of a learning *community*. I am seldom able to complete an entire crossword puzzle on my own. Once, for example, I was stuck on a seemingly simple puzzle. The four-letter clue was "Orpheus's instrument," and knowing from previous clues that the first letter was "L" and the last letter was "E," I had penciled in "LYRE." Unfortunately, the rest of the puzzle didn't fit. Eventually I gave up and handed the puzzle to my wife, a professional musician, who quickly changed "LYRE" to "LUTE." After that, the rest of the puzzle fell neatly into place. Similarly, at a Christian college, we depend on others to help us revise our worldview. That's why Christian colleges call themselves learning communities. Not only your professors but coaches, resident hall directors, and fellow students bring different perspectives and areas of expertise that can help you adjust and refine your own worldview.

> *Why does college matter to God? Because it prepares us to be image-bearers of God and effective agents of redemption in every corner of creation.*

Of course, all analogies are imperfect, and the crossword puzzle metaphor falls short in two important ways. First, solving a crossword puzzle has never, to my recollection, changed the way I live. A worldview, however, is intimately connected to behavior. That's why the Christian college ultimately seeks to produce graduates who not only apply a Christian worldview to their disciplines but who *live* their lives differently. As one educator has stated, a Christian college is a workshop in meaningful, intentional, robust Christian living. Discipleship, not intellectual analysis, is the goal of a Christian education.

Second, when I complete a crossword puzzle, I wad it up and throw it away. A worldview, however, is never fully complete. One doesn't spend four years of college constructing a worldview, then place it on the shelf and walk away. A Christian worldview helps us make sense of our lives and gives a sense of purpose to everything that we do, both individually and collectively. But just as Galileo's discoveries necessitated a change to the medieval worldview, so new insights and experiences require that we re-examine and adjust our Christian worldview throughout our lives, and alter our actions accordingly. In other words, the pencil is a permanent part of the mature Christian's toolkit, and the college years are a good time to learn to use it.

The cow in Gary Larson's comic was right to raise her head and ask why she was eating grass. But the fact is, grass is good for cows, and as far as I can tell they seem to like it. In fact, it's essential to their survival. So too, Christian college students should ask why they're investing significant time and effort in higher education; and they should ask the "why" question of every course that they take. Why does college matter to God? Because it prepares us to be image-bearers of God and effective agents of redemption in every corner of creation. This book will unpack and explain that notion more fully—but we'll begin with a brief look at where the notion of a Christian college came from in the first place.

A Note on Sources

The literature on Christian worldview and education is vast. Two standard older texts are Richard Middleton and Brian Walsh, *The Transforming Vision: Shaping a Christian Worldview* (InterVarsity, 1984) and James Sire, *The Universe Next Door* (InterVarsity, 1974). Recent works include David Naugle, *Worldview: History of a Concept* (Eerdmans, 2002) and Albert Wolters, *Creation Regained* (Eerdmans, 2005). More recently, James K. A. Smith has sought to ground the notion of worldview in the affections and in liturgical practice in *Desiring the Kingdom: Worship, Worldview, and Cultural Formation* (Baker Academic, 2009).

The observation that "worldview" involves knowing from the heart as well as the mind is found in George Pierson, "Evangelicals and Worldview Confusion," in Matt Bonzo and Michael Stevens, eds., *After Worldview: Christian Higher Education in Postmodern Worlds* (Dordt College Press, 2009). The quotations from *The Magician's Nephew* and from Dorothy Sayers are from David Naugle, "Worldview: History, Theology, Implications," in *After Worldview*, pages 26 and 6.

Questions for Reflection and Discussion

1. What worldviews have you encountered so far in your educational background? What actions revealed them?

2. What have been the main influences in your life so far in shaping your own worldview? What examples demonstrate their influence on you?

3. Other than professors, who do you anticipate having the most impact on your worldview during your college years? Why?

4. What beliefs that you have brought with you to college are written in "pen"? What beliefs are written in "pencil"?

5. How should we determine which of our beliefs are open to revision and which ones are not?

2 WHERE WE CAME FROM

A History of Christian Colleges in America

I met my future wife in college—in the first week, to be exact! After we met, some of the first questions we asked each other were, "Where are you from?" and "What is your family like?" That's because as everyone knows, one of the best ways to understand a person is to become familiar with his or her past.

The same principle applies to institutions. Anyone planning to spend the next four or five years at a Christian college should have some awareness of where these institutions came from and how they have been shaped over the past few hundred years. In the previous chapter, I briefly discussed the typical worldviews found at the University of Michigan such as scientific materialism and modern hedonism. It may be surprising, therefore, to learn that in the 1800s, Michigan was in many ways a thoroughly Christian institution. All of the university's professors affirmed the Christian faith, and President Henry Tappan delivered annual lectures entitled "Evidences of the Christian Religion." Students attended chapel every day and church twice on Sunday.

Michigan wasn't alone in American higher education. Harvard University's original motto, for example, was *Christo et Ecclesiae*—"for Christ and the Church." So what changed, and why? This chapter will explain the Christian vision behind American colleges, how that vision waned in the 1800s, and how today's Christian colleges attempt to forge a distinctively Christian approach to higher education. Of course, this narrative does not characterize in detail every institution of Christian higher education in the U.S. In particular, it leaves out Catholic universities, which were isolated from the cultural mainstream for much of American history and were nurtured by theological traditions that far pre-dated America's origins. Nevertheless, the notion that Christian academic institutions are engaged in something of a recovery project—in rebuilding a robust, academically-rigorous enterprise of higher education that makes a difference in the world—does describe many Christian colleges today.

Part One:
The Founding and Growth of Christian Colleges, 1600-1860

The story begins four hundred years ago. Among North America's first European settlers was a group of fervent Christians from England known as Puritans. When the main group of Puritans landed in New England in 1630, they immediately set about building shelter, planting crops, cooking Thanksgiving dinner with the local Indians, and doing other tasks necessary to survive in the North American wilderness. Not long after that—in 1636, to be exact—they founded Harvard College.

The Puritan movement was imbued with a fire for Christian thinking, and so founding a college in the harsh New England wilderness was second nature to them. Harvard College's primary purpose was to train pastors for the Puritan churches, but the college also educated New England's political and social leaders. As for coursework, the college placed a heavy emphasis on Latin, Greek, and Hebrew. It also stressed rhetoric, and to a lesser extent theology, ethics, politics, mathematics, and history. Bible instruction took place on Sunday, when Harvard students had to sit through two lengthy sermons and then repeat them to their tutors on Sunday evening.

For much of the 1600s, Harvard was the only institution in colonial higher education. In the next century, however, several new Christian colleges were established in the Harvard mold. In 1701, Connecticut Puritans, fearing that Harvard was departing from its Christian moorings, established Yale College. A few decades later, other denominations followed suit. Thus were born

Harvard College, 1740

many of America's Ivy League universities as we know them today—schools such as Princeton, Brown, and Dartmouth. Indeed, virtually without exception, American colleges begun in the colonial era were created by Protestants with the explicit purpose of training Christians to effectively engage their culture as leaders in the church and society.

This isn't to say that Christian education in the 1700s was a Golden Age by any means. In the classroom, professors typically employed the less-than-inspiring "recitation" method: Students memorized the lecture for the day and then regurgitated it back to a tutor. Some students, forced to attend college by socially-ambitious parents, livened up the dull routine by breaking rules, threatening professors, and rioting on occasion.

> *Virtually without exception, American colleges begun in the colonial era were created by Protestants with the explicit purpose of training Christian leaders for the church and society.*

However, for all of their shortcomings, Puritan colleges embodied an ideal that will be explored in further detail in subsequent chapters—that Christian thinking should embrace not just the Bible but should range over *all* subjects; that as God's image-bearers we are free to pursue truth in all areas. As the modern educator Henry Zylstra has put it in words that the Puritan founders would affirm, "In Christian education, nothing matters but the kingdom of Jesus Christ; but because of the kingdom, everything else matters." In other words, the Puritans made no distinction between "Christian" and "secular" subjects—it was all God's world out there for his creatures to explore and enjoy.

The Old-Time College

American Christians took a break from college-building in the late-1700s as the American Revolution took center stage. In the 1800s, however, a host of new colleges arrived on the scene. Some of these—Catholic universities—were an entirely new type, at least from the perspective of American Protestants. Roman Catholic immigrants did not arrive in the U.S. in large numbers until the late-1700s. Excluded from mainstream society, they quickly began building their own educational institutions, beginning with Georgetown University in 1791. Other Catholic colleges soon followed, including one, Notre Dame, that gladly adopted as its mascot the Protestants' stereotype of Catholic immigrants: the "Fighting Irish."

Protestants as well as Catholics engaged in college-building in the 1800s. Spurred on by a series of religious revivals known as the Second Great Awakening, they founded Christian colleges by the hundreds—over five hundred of them, to be exact, though only about two hundred survived into the twentieth century. For countless communities, establishing a Christian college was not so much a response to overwhelming demand for education as it was a way to assert a town's significance and community spirit. These schools came to be known as "Old-Time Colleges," and they had several features in common.

First, Old-Time Colleges exuded a strongly Christian ethos. College presidents were typically Christian ministers, and professors were expected to be generalists who could teach just about everything. The goal of the college curriculum was not so much to impart particular knowledge as to develop a mature, balanced Christian young person who thought clearly and behaved morally. This was best done, it was believed, through a balanced assortment of courses in literature, science, and the arts.

Concerning student life, the colleges operated *in loco parentis*—"in the place of parents"—and strictly regulated the lives of students. Colleges specified times for waking up, studying, attending classes, playing, and retiring. A host of rules governed student life, and daily chapel was required. "Amusement" such as Sabbath breaking, card-playing, alcohol, tobacco, foul language, and disorderly conduct were prohibited. As one might imagine, such strict supervision could at times spark resistance, and student riots were not uncommon. Princeton College, for example, experienced six separate riots between 1800 and 1830, one of which left the campus's main building, Nassau Hall, in ashes.

Old Brick Row, Yale College, 1807

As an antidote to student rebellion, colleges promoted revivals to heighten the religious fervor of the student body. Yale College was especially known for the intensity of its campus revivals. Throughout the 1800s Yale stood as the premier Christian college in the nation both in its academic quality and in the spiritual fervor of its students. Its graduates fanned out across the South and West, founding and presiding over new Christian colleges, thus earning Yale the reputation as the nineteenth century's "mother of colleges." Such religious characteristics were not limited to private colleges. As mentioned earlier, even most public universities of the day saw themselves as essentially Christian institutions.

In all, the colleges and universities in the mid-1800s, on the eve of the Civil War, reflected the beliefs and values of America's most dominant cultural group, white middle-class Protestants. Little did they realize that in a few decades, American university life would be almost completely secular and Christian colleges would be relegated to the cultural backwaters of society.

Part Two:
The Collapse and Revival of the Christian College, 1860 to 2000

To understand the swift collapse of Old-Time Colleges in the late-nineteenth century, we must explore these institutions more deeply. American Christian higher education in the 1800s seemed quite healthy, but this outward strength masked serious internal weaknesses. First, these institutions were essentially havens for a small group of privileged white males. Except for innovative Oberlin College and a few other institutions, women and African-Americans were largely excluded from nineteenth century colleges. In 1870, only 1.7 percent of American young people aged 18-21 were enrolled in colleges and universities. College was essentially a four-year rite of passage for members of the nation's privileged class before they took their positions in ministry, law, or medicine.

For anyone else in nineteenth-century America, college was largely perceived as impractical and irrelevant. The colleges maintained a rigid classical curriculum in which all students took the same classes throughout their four years of study. The system neglected the educational interests of some of the most productive members of society such as farmers, businessmen, and mechanics. As a result, many colleges went extinct, and those that survived were forced to keep student costs artificially low in order to maintain enrollment. College professors often bore the brunt of the colleges' financial problems, earning paltry salaries that barely kept them above the poverty level. Not that such professors were likely to earn higher pay elsewhere. Typically kindly old gentlemen, college professors hardly commanded respect as an intellectual force in society. Remarked the nineteenth century Bostonian Henry Adams about the professors in his day, "No one took Harvard College seriously."

Adams's remark points to the most serious weakness of the nineteenth century Christian college: Its lack of deep, intentional, rigorous Christian thinking across a range of subjects that had characterized the Puritans. As historian Mark Noll has noted, because Protestant educators' values fit so neatly with that of the surrounding society, they neglected to develop a clear Christian foundation for or critique of their cultural situation. They failed, in Noll's words, "to push thinking from the Scripture to modern situations and back again." For example, in a society in which the enslavement of black people was considered by most Americans to be acceptable, most Christian colleges failed to ask deep questions about how social norms did or did not reflect the will of God.

Because Protestant educators' values fit so neatly with that of the surrounding society, they neglected to develop a clear Christian foundation for or critique of their cultural situation.

In all, Protestants created colleges that promoted warm-hearted evangelical piety and the formation of moral character, but that generally failed to offer a well-rounded Christian approach to higher education. When dramatic changes hit American society in the late-1800s, the Old-Time Colleges found themselves to be built on shifting sand.

The Secularization of the University

The first major development to affect Christian colleges was a change in the nature of science. Nineteenth-century Christians had believed that doing science was simply a matter of organizing one's observations of the natural world into general laws that revealed God's goodness and purpose in creation—that, in other words, science always confirmed the Bible. By the mid-1800s, however, new views of science emerging in Europe challenged this notion. Scientists, European scholars asserted, should be guided by the assumption that all phenomena originated from natural, not supernatural, causes. The task of the scientist, therefore, was to trace events to their natural causes, thereby excluding any considerations of God's design and activity in creation.

Charles Darwin's theory of evolution, which was publicized in 1859, was both a product of and a catalyst for this new intellectual trend. Darwin argued that humans were not created by God but rather evolved through random changes over millions of years. Such a theory seemed to contradict Christians' belief in the literal truth of Genesis as well as the comforting notion that science revealed evidence of God's handiwork in nature. Christians who had assured themselves that science invariably supported Christian belief could offer little by way of effective response now that science seemed to point in the opposite direction.

The Cornell University Library, 1891

At the same time that scientists were questioning Christian intellectual foundations, vast new financial sources for modern universities emerged that dwarfed the budgets of the Old-Time Colleges. In 1862, Congress passed the Morrill Act, which made

government funds available for states to establish public universities, such as Michigan State and Texas A & M, that would advance practical education in the areas of agriculture and mechanics.
Government support for higher education was joined by private do-
nations. The industrial society of the late-1800s produced fabulously
wealthy men such as Ezra Cornell, Johns Hopkins, and Cornelius
Vanderbilt. These industrialists poured huge sums of money into
universities bearing their names, both as a means of boosting their
own stature and to generate the scientific discoveries and technological know-how needed by the new industrial society.

Thus was born the modern public research university that has
become a fixture in modern America, and which vastly overshad-
owed the pre-Civil War Christian college in size, money, and social
prominence. Where the Old-Time College counted its students in
the hundreds, the new universities educated thousands. In 1850,
for example, about 28,000 Americans were enrolled in college—
far fewer than the 72,000 spectators who filled Michigan Stadium,
built in the early 1900s, to watch the Wolverines play college football on a Saturday afternoon. In 1824, Princeton College was considered audacious when it sought to raise $100,000 from its alumni.
A half-century later, Johns Hopkins, a banker and investor in the
Baltimore & Ohio Railroad, personally donated $3.5 million to es-
tablish a German-style research university.

Rather than employing retired, underpaid ministers to teach
everything from geometry to ancient history, the modern university employed trained experts in particular fields. The Ph.D., not
personal piety, became the most desirable quality in professors. The
new universities changed what students studied as well. In 1870,

> *Amid the specialized departments of the modern university, the attempt to understand a unified world of knowledge largely disappeared.*

Harvard president Charles Eliot discarded the college's traditional classical curriculum and introduced the elective system, whereby students chose their own course of study from a number of different subjects and departments. Eliot's innovation proved so successful in attracting students that other universities soon followed suit. By the end of the century the classical curriculum was rapidly disappearing in American higher education.

Like most big changes that occur in history, the rise of the secular research university was neither all bad nor all good. Clearly the new universities brought about academic and social improvements. They expressed a basic Christian belief that education should affect the way we live and bring about positive changes in culture. But amid the specialized departments of the modern university, the attempt to understand and present a unified world of knowledge largely disappeared. Moreover, the traditional Christian college's concern for molding the character of its students—for linking head and heart—gradually evaporated. The modern university was a secular enterprise designed to produce competency in a professional and technological society; Christian perspectives that got in the way of progress and impeded scientific advances were excluded outright or pushed to the margins of university life.

So how did Christians in higher education respond to these new developments? Generally in two ways, neither of which were adequate. First, many Christian colleges sought to keep up with the new trends by abandoning or obscuring their religious identity. Rather than discarding Christian belief immediately, such colleges typically redefined Christianity as simply devotion to high moral ideals or service to humanity. Eventually, even the Christian rhetoric disappeared as these institutions became smaller versions of the secular research university. Thus, college chapels and campus inscriptions such as Harvard's *Christo et Ecclesiae* function largely as vestiges of a bygone era in American higher education.

Of course, not all Americans abandoned Christian higher education in the late-1800s. Catholic universities remained largely unaffected by the secularizing tendencies of the day. Furthermore, many Protestant colleges with close connections to denominations such as Baptists, Lutherans, and Mennonites sustained a

The Harvard Seal, 1700   The Harvard Seal, 1900

commitment to Christian higher education. But within the mainstream Protestant colleges, especially those without strong denominational ties, a more defensive, anti-intellectual posture tended to take root. Conservative evangelical Christians at the turn of the century feared that American culture was slipping from its Christian foundations, and that applied to the nation's colleges. "Christian schools were once the pride of our nation," exclaimed the pastor T. C. Horton. "Now, many are the progeny of Satan." Thus, conservatives transformed existing institutions such as Wheaton College in Illinois and created "Bible colleges" such as the Bible Institute of Los Angeles (BIOLA) to provide a Christian education that they believed was disappearing in the culture at large.

These "evangelical" colleges admirably strove to provide a semblance of Christian education in a secularizing age. However, as well-rounded Christian intellectual institutions they displayed serious shortcomings. Bible colleges sought to provide brief, practical training for young people who planned to become full-time Christian workers. This emphasis on "practical" Christian education led such institutions to neglect an interest in a wide range of subjects and academic disciplines. As historian Virginia Brereton has observed, "general education was considered an unwanted extravagance given the exigencies of the time." The Bible college's focus on evangelism and missions tended to crowd out a healthy interest in all of God's creation that the Puritan colleges had displayed.

Furthermore, many conservative Christians in the early twentieth century developed a preoccupation with end-of-the-world biblical prophecy—especially the belief in an imminent "rapture" of believers to heaven—which led them to de-emphasize attention to the affairs of the visible world. Why study politics or biology, they wondered, if the world is about to end soon anyway? "Secular" learning came to be seen as either a set of false ideas to be refuted or as dangerous to the beliefs of Christian young people and thus best left alone. Subjects such as the Bible, apologetics, and evangelism seemed safer and more practical.

In all, Christian colleges exchanged one overly-simplistic approach to American culture with another: While Christian colleges in the 1800s tended to assume that they had a privileged role of *dominance* in American culture, the evangelical colleges of the 1900s sought *separation* from their surrounding culture. Thus, while Christian higher education in the twentieth century continued on in the wake of secularization, in many cases it was only a shadow of the robust vision articulated by earlier Christians such as the Puritans.

Reviving Christian Higher Education

In recent decades, however, evangelical colleges have been growing in size, quality, and awareness of their cultural calling. Part of their revival is due to the growth of American conservative Christianity in general. While liberal Protestantism has declined in the past half-century, evangelical churches have increased in size and resources. Thus, there are more students available to populate evangelical colleges, and financially successful Christians have more money to invest in them. In 1976, thirty-eight intentionally Christ-centered colleges in the U.S. joined together to form the Council for Christian College and Universities (CCCU). The organization now has over one hundred members and seventy-three affiliates in twenty-four different nations that collectively enroll over 300,000 students. Enrollment in CCCU institutions increased 70% in the years from 1990 to 2004—far outpacing the growth of American higher education in general.

Moreover, Christian colleges have witnessed a revival of concern for breadth of learning in all disciplines. The catalyst for this recovery was Abraham Kuyper, a nineteenth-century Dutch theologian and politician. Kuyper urged Christians of his day to engage their culture, and he articulated an approach to learning in which Christian truths were integrated into all academic disciplines. As Kuyper put it, "There is not a square inch on the whole plain of human existence over which Christ, who is Lord over all, does not proclaim, 'This is Mine!'" In Kuyper's philosophy, chemistry, psychology, history, and sociology had as much place in the Christian college curriculum as theology and philosophy. Moreover, Kuyper sought to *integrate* Christian faith with learning in every discipline.

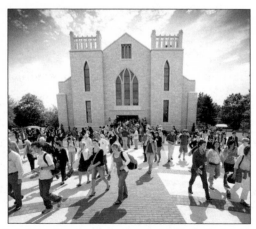

Cathedral of the Ozarks on the campus of John Brown University

Kuyper's educational approach impacted Calvin College, a Dutch Reformed school in Michigan, in the mid-twentieth century. Later, when several colleges joined with Calvin to form the Christian College Coalition, Kuyper's influence spread throughout American Christian higher education. Eventually it even impacted major universities such as Notre Dame and Baylor when former Calvin College professors nurtured in Kuyper's worldview assumed influential faculty positions at those institutions. By the 1980s, the "integration" model of faith and learning, which we will explore in chapter six, had come to permeate many Christian colleges, prompting them to pursue a distinctively Christian approach to learning.

> *By the 1980s, the "integration" model of faith and learning had become standard fare among Christian Colleges, inspiring them to pursue broad academic excellence and a distinctively Christian approach to learning.*

Thus, the Christian college in America today represents something different than simply a return to the Old-Time College of the 1800s. For one thing, the nineteenth-century model of the professor as a kindly old "jack of all trades" may have encouraged the development of Christian character, but it did not always challenge students to love God with their minds. The typical Christian college professor today is both a mentor who cares about the spiritual development of students and a qualified scholar in his or her academic discipline. One important lesson of the past two centuries is that it was not too much thinking that led colleges to secularize; rather, it was a lack of clear, rigorous Christian thinking applied to the wide range of emerging academic disciplines that led institutions to see Christianity as basically irrelevant to their mission. Christian professors who combine spiritual commitment and academic excellence make secularization less likely.

Second, the elaborate lists of rules and restrictions on students' lives that characterized nineteenth century colleges have grown shorter over the years. Christian educators today do not see their role as primarily *in loco parentis* but rather that of helping to form students into mature Christians who demonstrate wisdom and own their faith for themselves. Thus, Christian colleges in their lifestyle expectations generally seek a greater balance between community standards and personal freedom.

Finally, modern Christian colleges display a more flexible course of study than those of the past. The nineteenth-century college curriculum rooted in the classics, while valuable, made no allowance for a student's unique intellectual interests and career goals. Today's Christian college recognizes that part of its mission is to equip students to effectively engage their culture as Christians in their profession. Thus, it typically combines required classes in the Christian liberal arts with more professionally oriented studies in a major of one's choice.

Of course, Christian colleges are by no means perfect. Especially in difficult economic times, many of them struggle to enroll enough students to maintain healthy budgets. Moreover, faculty and student accomplishments at secular universities—not to mention financial resources—often exceed those of Christian colleges. Nevertheless, these colleges have managed to maintain a commitment to distinctive Christian education, even when that vision was challenged by the broader society and when many leading institutions abandoned such a vision. The next few chapters will explore how the basic elements of the Christian story make a profound difference to college.

A Note on Sources

There are a number of excellent historical works that detail the history of American Christian colleges and American Christian thinking in general. Among the best are George Marsden's *The Soul of the American University* (Oxford, 1994), William Ringenberg's *The Christian College* (Eerdmans, 2006), James Burtchaell's *The Dying of the Light* (Eerdmans, 1998), Joel Carpenter's and Kenneth Shipps' *Making Higher Education Christian* (Eerdmans, 1987), Richard Hughes's and William Adrian's *Models for Christian Higher Education* (Eerdmans, 1997), and Mark Noll's *The Scandal of the Evangelical Mind* (Eerdmans, 1994). Somewhat older, but still useful, is Frederick Rudolph's *The American College and University: A History* (Vintage Books, 1962).

Henry Zylstra is quoted in Henry Beversluis's "Toward a Theology of Education" (Calvin College Papers, February, 1981), 10. A discussion of student riots is found in Frederick Rudolph, *The American College*, 96-99. Statistics concerning nineteenth century higher education are drawn from Rudolph, 486 and the 1854 United States Census. Henry Adams's quote comes from Mark Noll's introduction to William Ringenberg's *The Christian College*, 17. Noll's discussion of the weaknesses in nineteenth century Christian thought is found in his book The Scandal of the Evangelical Mind, 107. T. C. Horton is quoted in the *Ozark American* (September, 1922), 11. Virginia Brereton's remark is found in her book *Training God's Army: The American Bible School, 1880-1940* (Indiana University Press, 1990), 115. Kuyper's statement is quoted in James Bratt and Ronald Wells, "Piety and Progress: A History of Calvin College," in Richard Hughes and William Adrian, eds., *Models for Christian Higher Education*, 143.

Questions for Reflection and Discussion

1. Do you think that the process of Christian colleges "going secular" is inevitable? Why or why not?

2. What features of Christian colleges of the past are worth emulating today? Which ones are not?

3. What could the colleges of the 1800s have done to avoid becoming secularized?

4. Can Christian colleges de-emphasize rules and still be distinctively Christian? If so, how?

5. What do you think is the value of a network of Christian colleges that is broader than any one single institution?

3   LIVING LARGELY

The Doctrine of Creation

DAVID Brisben, a friend of mine who teaches theology, grew up in the South as part of the post-World War II baby boomer generation. Each evening, David recalls, after the five o'clock supper, David's father would announce that it was "homework time." To justify his orders, David's father, a mill-worker, would declare to his four children that he wanted all of them to "do better than he had done"—that is, his children would go to college and land "well-paying jobs." After all, the South Carolina Department of Education had declared on highway billboards across the state, "To get a good job, get a good education." For David's father, and for many parents like him, higher education was the pathway to higher paying jobs, nicer homes, newer cars, and better vacations. It was the key to having one's children do better in life.

Such thinking is not unique. Since World War II, a college education in America has been billed as the means to social and economic mobility. That trend continues today. As professors William Willimon and Thomas Naylor document in their book, *The Abandoned Generation*, the purpose of higher education has been to help students realize their economic potential, or put more crassly, "to become a money-making machine." Modern universities certainly encourage this way of thinking, and college freshmen readily confess that they are attending college to improve their economic potential. Some can even confidently predict how much more earning power they will have than their high school friends who do not to go to college.

This kind of thinking is not completely off the mark. Christians certainly would agree that there is value in emphasizing career development. The ancient Hebrews, moreover, believed that part of a parent's responsibility included equipping their children with life skills or what today is called "career development." As we saw earlier, one of the weaknesses of nineteenth-century colleges was their refusal to develop programs of education that would train the hands of students as well as educate their heads. Hence, at Christian colleges today, admissions counselors, career development officers, and student development leaders promote the economic value of a college education.

Nevertheless, Christian colleges stand in opposition to modern culture's understanding of college in some important ways. First, Christians do not believe that it's necessary to go to college in order to experience "the good life." A fascinating book by Matthew Crawford, entitled *Shop Class as Soulcraft*, makes this point well. Crawford completed a Ph.D. in political philosophy from the University of Chicago and went on to direct a think tank. He then resigned his position to start a motorcycle repair shop. He discovered more intellectual challenge and emotional satisfaction in the task of repairing engines than in creating ideas. Crawford's point is one that Christians, who believe that all human work is noble, should endorse: Humans are made for excellence, and they can fulfill that calling in a variety of tasks, some of which require a college education and some of which don't. In other words, college isn't for everyone.

Second, Christian colleges do more than simply prepare students for successful careers. In some cases, college will equip you to critique and *transform* your profession, not just succeed in it (more about that in chapter five). Finally, Christian colleges are founded on the notion that education isn't simply a commodity to be purchased or a tool to be used for career success. Rather, for Christians learning is an *intrinsic* good rooted in the doctrine of creation. To explore this idea, let's look at part of the creation story as recorded in Genesis 1:

Career development by itself is an inadequate purpose for higher education. Rather, for Christians learning is an intrinsic good rooted in the doctrine of creation.

> Then God said, "Let us make man in our own image, in our likeness, and let them rule over the fish of the sea and the birds of the air, over the livestock, over all the earth, and over all the creatures that move along the ground." So God created man in his own image, in the image of God he created him; male and female he created them. God blessed them and said to them, "Be fruitful and increase in number; fill the earth and subdue it. Rule over the fish of the sea and the birds of the air and over every living creature that moves on the ground." . . . And God saw all that he had made, and it was very good.

Modern Christians have debated at length over how to interpret the early chapters of Genesis. Were the "days" of creation literal twenty-four-hour days? Did God create every species individually, or did some species evolve from others under God's sovereign guidance? During your college years, you will likely have ample opportunity to discuss such questions. But for now, our purpose is to understand the central message of this creation story and how it applies to our lives at a Christian college. In sum, the biblical creation account has four key implications for education.

1. We know God better by studying his creation.

The personality of the sculptor comes through in the sculpture. Similarly, as Creator, God expresses himself in all that he has made, and what he made reveals and declares important things about him. This truth helps us better appreciate why Adam, as representative of humanity, was given the task of naming the animals. Genesis 2 contains this rather startling passage: "Now the Lord God had formed out of the ground all the beasts of the field and all the birds of the air. He brought them to the man to see what he would name them; and whatever the man called each living creature, that was its name." I suspect that the biblical narrator writes this passage with a touch of humor. Why would the Creator of the universe grant to Adam, this upstart creature, the responsibility of bestowing names on all of the living creatures? Did God really wait in suspense to see what names Adam would come up with? Did God know that "platypus" and "dodo bird" would eventually result?

For the ancient Hebrews, to "name" something meant far more than it does to modern Americans. It meant to understand it deeply, to know the characteristics of the thing named. In other words, God was bringing his creatures to Adam so that Adam could share in God's knowledge of his creation. Adam was to reflect knowing and understanding the animals the way the Creator knows and understands them. In doing so, he would not only reflect the knowledge and wisdom of his Creator, but also know God in a deeper, more profound way. "Naming" a tiger, for example, would help Adam understand and appreciate the beauty and power of God's creation. Adam's encounter with an otter, by contrast, would teach him something about the Creator's own playfulness and sense of humor. By extension, then, "naming the animals" is what happens whenever we study God's creation. It is what botanists do when they discover a new plant species, or what astronomers do when they discover a new galaxy and put a name on it.

When we move from Genesis to the New Testament, we learn that creation itself was the work of Jesus Christ. As Paul writes in his letter to the Colossians: "For by him all things were created: things in heaven and on earth, visible and invisible, whether thrones or powers or rulers of authorities; all things were created by him and for him." To study the created world, therefore, is to study the works of Christ himself.

> *Because Christians begin the educational task with the understanding that the entire universe is God's creation, learning new subjects is never simply about acquiring more information.*

Because Christians begin the educational task with the understanding that the entire universe is Christ's creation, learning new subjects is never simply about acquiring more information. It's a way to know Christ better and more deeply love him. As John Piper notes, "everything—from the bottom of the oceans to the top of the mountains, from the smallest particle to the biggest star, from the most boring school subject to the most fascinating science, from the ugliest cockroach to the most beautiful human, . . . exists to make the greatness of Christ more fully known." A class in cell biology isn't just a preparation for the next stage of a pre-med program; properly understood, it's actually a way to deepen one's relationship with Christ, the Creator of cells.

2. We are called to care for and *develop* God's creation.

Genesis tells us that God intended human beings not just to "name" his creation but to rule over it and develop it. Christians often are so used to rushing on to the serpent and apple episode that they fail to ask an important question of the creation story: What would Adam and Eve have done with their lives if they hadn't sinned and been kicked out of Eden? After all, one suspects that sitting around eating fruit and naming animals would have grown tedious after a while.

So what was God's original purpose for his image-bearers? Genesis 1 and 2 give us a clue: "God blessed them and said to them, 'Be fruitful and increase in number; fill the earth and subdue it. Rule over the fish of the sea and the birds of the air and over every living creature that moves on the ground.'" And a few verses later: "The Lord God took the man and put him in the Garden of Eden to work it and take care of it." Many of us have read these passages so often that we miss their significance. Isn't God going a bit far, entrusting his glorious new creation to such frail creatures? Isn't it a bit like a father giving the keys to his new Ferrari convertible to his sixteen-year-old son? Indeed, one of the astounding truths of Genesis 1 and 2 is that God gives Adam and Eve tremendous responsibilities to rule over and care for his creation.

A good ruler, of course, does not just sit on a throne. The ruler actively *develops* the kingdom—bringing improvements, solving disputes, and increasing prosperity. And that is the privilege God entrusted to humans. From the very beginning, humans were expected to bring changes to creation. Some sort of transformation was to take place as part of cultivating and caring for the earth. Theologians refer to this task as the "cultural mandate"—that God created humans not only to enjoy his creation, but to develop it, even to transform it. Consider the opposite end of the Bible, the book of Revelation. This book tells us that the culmination of God's redemptive work will not be another garden but rather a city—and not an ordinary city but one with walls decorated with precious jewels, streets of gold, and full of gardens and vineyards. If Genesis depicts a creation as simple and harmonious as a Bach cello solo, Revelation describes a complex, multi-layered creation like that of a Beethoven symphony.

So how do we get from the Garden to the Heavenly City? By human beings actively and creatively cultivating God's creation. We often associate the word "culture" with particular forms such as art, music, and dance—hence we call a person "cultured" who is knowledgeable about such things. But as Andy Crouch reminds us in *Culture Making,* culture is simply "what we make of the world." By implication, therefore, everything humans do, from making an omelet to designing a car, is an act of making culture that fulfills God's original good purpose for his creation.

The importance of developing God's creation is reinforced when one moves to the New Testament and the person of Christ—namely, the doctrine of the Incarnation. The fact that Jesus Christ, while fully God, took on actual flesh and blood means that the material stuff of creation is not to be avoided but valued. Christians of all people should appreciate the fact that the world that Christ chose to inhabit, though fallen, still holds the potential for great beauty and complexity.

One of the purposes of a college education, therefore, is to equip us to cultivate God's good creation more lovingly and effectively. The study of engineering, for example, helps us to learn how to build bridges that span rivers. Architecture teaches us how to construct more efficient and comfortable buildings. Graphic design teaches us how to create objects that communicate with clarity and aesthetic appeal. Business helps us develop healthy economic relationships that are essential to any complex society. A course in English helps us use language in creative new ways. And the list goes on. Many of your college courses, and particularly your major, will prepare you to assume your God-given role as a fellow-cultivator of creation.

> *Many of your college courses, and particularly your major, will prepare you to assume your God-given role as a fellow-cultivator of creation.*

3. The study of creation includes the insights of non-believers.

There is a popular slogan at Christian colleges: "All truth is God's truth, wherever it may be found." Over the next few years you may grow weary of hearing this remark, but it's true nonetheless. Because God created all that exists and called it good, all aspects of creation are worth studying. Thus, a Christian college does not limit itself to studying only Christian writers and Christian ideas. We study a variety of academic subjects and scholars, even non-Christians—not just to refute their ideas but to learn from them.

How can this be true? One implication of the creation story is the doctrine of "common grace," that is, that God has liberally sprinkled his grace over all of his creation, and that the effects of God's grace persist even after the fall. In other words, even non-Christian scholars can have insights into truths about the universe. The atheistic scientists James Watson and Francis Crick, for example, were the first researchers to discern the structure of DNA. They did so by diligently studying creation, not by reading the Bible. John Calvin likened the non-Christian scholar's situation to that of "a traveler passing through a field at night who in a momentary lightning flash sees far and wide, but the sight vanishes so swiftly that he is plunged again into the darkness of the night before he can take even a step." We may disagree with Calvin over the extent to which the non-Christian is "plunged again into darkness," but his lightning metaphor is helpful nonetheless.

A scholar such as Sigmund Freud, for example, may have been wrong about the general truths of God's personal existence and humanity's divine spark. But his experiments and explorations of the

subconscious yield helpful insights into the human psyche for non
-Christians and Christians alike. Freud's writings may be potentially
threatening to a young Christian raised in a sheltered environment,
but they are still worth taking seriously and can teach us valuable
truths. Because God's common grace is spread throughout creation,
we can expect to find new truths in all sorts of unlikely places. As
a result, the Christian college does not insulate students from the
ideas of non-Christian scholars but seeks to understand those ideas
within a larger Christian framework.

4. We glorify God by taking delight in his creation.

Participating in God's creation involves not just the intellect but
the emotions. That is because humans were created to experience
the same kind of joy and delight in the creation that the Creator
himself experiences. God revels in his creation, enjoys it, and loves
it. Genesis 1 informs us repeatedly that God took great delight
in his creative activity and called it good. The importance of this
truth—God delighting in his creation—is reinforced throughout the
Scriptures. In Job 38-41, for example, God tells Job that he plays
with large sea creatures; he boasts about the rivers he creates, the
storehouses of snow that he keeps, and the understanding he gives
to the different creatures.

It is hard to read these chapters and not picture a child at play;
but then play also comes from God. Of all the creatures, Genesis
tells us, humans alone were created in God's image. We alone were
created expressly to be like God. Theologians call this concept the
imago dei—the image of God. And while theologians continue to
debate the full meaning of this expression, they do agree that it

means that we have been uniquely created to understand, to think about, to delight in, and to enjoy the creation the way God does.

Here's an analogy: Picture a father painstakingly constructing a swing-set for his children. His effort is motivated by the expectation of seeing their joy and hearing their laughter when they jump off the swings and slide down the slide. Their enjoyment of the swing-set not only reflects the father's own affinity for play, but it also expresses their gratitude and admiration for his handiwork. Similarly, when we admire the Grand Canyon, kayak a mountain stream, or cook a savory meal, we express the reality of the *imago dei* and bring pleasure to the Creator of these things.

This concept of human beings created to delight in God's creation gives further purpose to a Christian college. That's because the beauty of God's creation is not limited to the natural world; we experience it in human culture as well. Poets, artists, philosophers, and even mathematicians discover and develop parts of creation that delight the imagination and feed the soul. I once saw a documentary about a Princeton mathematician who proved a geometrical concept called Fermat's last theorem. He literally broke down in tears as he described

> *We have been uniquely created to think about, to delight in, and to enjoy the creation the way God does. When we admire the Grand Canyon, kayak a mountain stream, or cook a savory meal, we express the reality of the* imago dei.

the moment of discovery and the "indescribable beauty" and simplicity of the proof.

One of the purposes of a Christian college, therefore, is to help us develop the ability not just to understand but to delight in God's creation. A child can enjoy Beethoven's Fifth Symphony, especially when it accompanies a Bugs Bunny cartoon. But the person who has studied music theory, music history, and the life of Beethoven can appreciate the symphony in a far deeper way. Similarly, the graduate of a course in Astronomy can enjoy the beauty of the stars in a deeper way than the person who simply recognizes the Big Dipper in the night sky. In other words, higher education develops our ability to glorify God by enjoying his creation in all of its variety and depth.

All of this can be summed up in the notion of education as an *intrinsic* good, or good for its own sake. We can think of objects as having either instrumental or intrinsic value. A shovel, for example, is a tool that has instrumental value. We don't mount it on our wall to admire; we use it to dig a hole. The *Mona Lisa*, by contrast, is good for its own sake, not for any use that we would put it to. Similarly, a beautiful sunset is an intrinsic good. We admire it for itself, not for any practical purpose that it could be put to. When it comes to education, the secular world typically views college in instrumental terms: A college education "pays off" in a more lucrative and satisfying career. Christians, however, begin with the understanding that learning has intrinsic value regardless of whatever practical benefits it might produce. God created all things, and he created us in his image to explore and delight in his creation.

It's popular nowadays to turn nouns into verbs. For example, we don't just read a text. Rather, we *text* a colleague on our cell phone;

or we *friend* someone on Facebook. In conclusion, it may be helpful to think of *image* as a verb rather than a noun. That is, because of the doctrine of *imago dei*, as Christians one of our chief callings in life is to "image" God. Clifford Williams, in his book *The Life of the Mind*, coins the term "living largely" to describe our calling as God's image-bearers. Too many Christians, he says, live constricted lives. They miss the wideness of experiences that comes to those who are open to new possibilities. Living a constricted life is like reading Harlequin romances instead of Jane Austen, or drinking grape Kool-Aid rather than French wine. When we live largely, however, we actively look for fresh ways to experience the richness and goodness of God's creation. In other words, we "image" God better and more deeply as we engage in his creation.

Regardless of the particular major that one studies, college, at its most basic level, prepares us to image God throughout all of life. God creates; as his image-bearer, I sub-create. Studying art and music enables me to be a better creator. Studying history enables me to better understand how humans have cultivated the "garden" of civilization over time. Every book I read, mathematical equation I wrestle with, or painting I experience expands me, and by extension my ability to "image" God. Reading English literature may or may not make me love God more, but it gives me *more* to love God *with*.

As we'll see in the next chapter, the world is messed up in some big ways. But that fact shouldn't blind us to the goodness that still pervades God's creation and our opportunity as image-bearers of God to understand, develop, and delight in that creation. A Christian college education enables us to do that in deeper and richer ways.

A Note on Sources

All Scripture references are from the New International Version. Willimon and Taylor's observation about college students as "money-making machines" is found in *The Abandoned Generation* (Eerdmans, 1995), 39. John Calvin's remark about common grace is found in the article "Why God Enjoys Baseball," by David Neff (*Christianity Today*, July 8, 2002). Two of the best sources for reading more about the doctrine of creation and education are Andy Crouch's *Culture Making: Recovering Our Creative Calling* (InterVarsity, 2008) and Clifford Williams' *The Life of the Mind* (Baker, 2002). A more recent book connecting the value of learning to Jesus Christ is Mark Noll's *Jesus Christ and the Life of the Mind* (Eerdmans, 2010). John Piper's remark is from Noll, 28.

The discussion of learning as an intrinsic good comes largely from Williams, chapter 2. Also, I am indebted to David Brisben, chair of the Biblical Studies department at John Brown University, for many of the ideas in this chapter.

Questions for Reflection and Discussion

1. If every college course is an opportunity to know God better, why is it often difficult to be motivated to learn and study?

2. What is a particular way that the "cultural mandate" would apply to your major?

3. Is it possible for Christian colleges to both equip students to "delight in God's creation," and to prepare them for a career? Why or not?

4. What is one course that you are taking this semester that will enable you to "live largely"? How, specifically, will it do so?

5. Could a non-Christian pursue education for its intrinsic value? Why or why not?

4 NOT THE WAY IT'S SUPPOSED TO BE

The Doctrine of the Fall

ONE of the best films of the 1990s was a little-known movie called *Grand Canyon*. It used the physical feature of the Grand Canyon as a metaphor for the racial and social divisions in America, and it depicted two Los Angeles families as they sought to bridge the divide. In the opening scene a wealthy white Los Angeles businessman, played by Kevin Kline, attempts to take a short cut home from a Lakers game late at night, only to have his BMW break down in a run-down neighborhood. He calls for a tow truck, but before the tow truck arrives, Kline is surrounded by a group of black teenagers who plan to steal his car. The tow truck driver, played by Danny Glover, arrives during a tense standoff between Kevin Kline and the black youths. Glover talks with the head of the gang, asking that he be allowed to tow the car—and Kevin Kline—to safety.

At the end of their conversation, Glover exclaims to the youth, "Man, the world ain't supposed to work like this. Maybe you don't know that, but this ain't the way it's supposed to be. I'm supposed to be able to do my job without asking you if I can. That dude's supposed to be able to wait with his car without you ripping him off."

> *Sin entered the world through Adam and Eve, and its effects spread throughout all of God's creation. What we see around us today is a distorted version of the beautiful, harmonious world that God created.*

He concludes with the memorable line, "Everything's supposed to be different than what it is."

Glover could have cited more examples: In a world "the way it's supposed to be," cities aren't divided between white and black neighborhoods. Wealth isn't divided between a few "haves" and a host of "have-nots." Urban youths don't form gangs and resort to crime and violence as their only way to escape poverty. Cars don't break down at inopportune times. In fact, Glover's soliloquy aptly sums up the biblical doctrine of the Fall: Sin entered the world through Adam and Eve, and its effects spread throughout all of God's creation. What we see around us today is a distorted version of the beautiful, harmonious world that God created. In this chapter we'll return to the biblical story of the Fall, then explore its implications for education.

Genesis 3 tells a story that is familiar to most of us in Western culture. God places Adam and Eve in the Garden of Eden and commands them not to eat from the "tree of the knowledge of good and evil." Which, of course, is exactly what they do:

> When the woman saw that the fruit of the tree was good for
> food and pleasing to the eye, and also desirable for gaining

wisdom, she took some and ate it. She also gave some to her husband, who was with her, and he ate it. Then the eyes of both of them were opened and they realized they were naked; so they sewed fig leaves together and made coverings for themselves. (3:6-7)

I recall encountering this story in Sunday School when I was growing up. The basic lesson was that sin created a gulf between humanity and God and made it necessary for Jesus Christ to die for our sins to restore that relationship. What I didn't understand at the time was that "the Fall," as theologians call it, disrupted not only human beings' relationship with God but in some mysterious way impacted all of God's creation. As Michael Wittmer observes in his book *Heaven Is a Place on Earth*, "Adam's sin did not just affect him but, like a stone tossed into a pond, rippled out until it had destroyed the entire world."

First, and most obviously, Adam and Eve's disobedience corrupted human relationships. Suddenly they realized that they were naked and sought to cover themselves with fig leaves. Soon the finger-pointing began. When God asks Adam if he ate from the tree, Adam replies, "The woman you put here with me—she gave me some fruit from the tree and I ate it" (3:12). Things quickly get much worse. Their son Cain, jealous over the favor that God shows to his brother Abel, kills Abel and is forced to flee for his life. In fact, the next few chapters depict the ripple effects of the Fall throughout human society, until the writer of Genesis states in chapter six: "The Lord saw how great man's wickedness on the earth had become, and that every inclination of the thoughts of his heart was only evil all the time. The Lord was grieved that he had made man on the earth, and his heart was filled with pain" (6:6). Quite the tragic contrast from the Creator who delighted in the goodness of his creation.

Adam and Eve's disobedience altered not only human society but the natural world as well. After Adam ate the forbidden fruit, God said to him, "Cursed is the ground because of you; through painful toil you will eat of it all the days of your life. It will produce thorns and thistles for you" (3:17). The pleasurable cultivation of the Garden that was Adam's original task has now been reduced to the drudgery of hacking at hard soil to extract some edible crops. Even the animal world gets implicated in the mess. In Genesis 6, God sends the flood not just to do away with humans but also with the rest of creation: "So the Lord said, 'I will wipe mankind, whom I have created, from the face of the earth—men and animals, and creatures that move along the ground, and the birds of the air—for I am grieved that I have made them'" (6:7).

In the New Testament, the Apostle Paul aptly describes the cosmic nature of the Fall when he writes, "The whole creation has been groaning as in the pains of childbirth right up to the present time" (Romans 8:22). In some mysterious way, all of creation has become disfigured by effects of the Fall so that what we see around us today is, as Danny Glover remarked, "not the way it's supposed to be."

Much more can be said about the Christian doctrine of the Fall. Indeed, volumes have been written over the centuries exploring how evil relates to divine sovereignty and human free will, how "original sin" spread, whether death in the natural world is a result of the fall, and a host of other related issues. You will probably navigate these rough waters at some point in your college career. Our purpose, however, is not to discuss the Fall in exhaustive detail but to look at Christian education through the lens of this foundational belief. So what does the Fall have to do with college? Here are some implications.

1. The Fall and the goodness of creation

First, it's important to consider what the Fall does *not* mean. The evil that we see in the world is *not* consonant with the creation itself. In other words, the goodness of God's creation that was discussed in the previous chapter persists despite its disfigurement by sin. One author has likened evil to a parasite on creation. That's a good analogy, since like a tapeworm in a dog's intestine, evil depends on a pre-existing good for its very existence. Moreover, as C. S. Lewis noted in *Mere Christianity*, it is the highest parts of creation that have the potential for the greatest evil: "The better stuff a creature is made of—the cleverer and stronger and freer it is—then the better it will be if it goes right, but also the worse it will be if it goes wrong."

This fact is important to keep in mind because sometimes Christians have demonstrated a tendency to identify evil with certain parts of creation itself, rather than as a corruption of creation, and

> *"The better stuff a creature is made of—the cleverer and stronger and freer it is—then the better it will be if it goes right, but also the worse it will be if it goes wrong."*
>
> C. S. Lewis

thus to avoid them altogether. For some, it was sex; or certain foods and drinks; or "worldly amusements" such as movies and cards; or politics. Yet many of the evils that Christians perceive in the world are actually distortions of some of creation's basic goods. God's good gift of sex becomes twisted into adultery or prostitution. Wine is distorted into drunkenness. Even a corrupt dictatorship depends for its existence on the prior good of political institutions that God established.

As noted in the previous chapter, one of the basic doctrines of Christianity is the Incarnation—that in the person of Jesus Christ, God took on human flesh and lived an earthly existence. As Christians through the centuries have pointed out, the Incarnation implies that the basic stuff of creation is good, and even though it is corrupted, it is still redeemable. Furthermore, God's common grace continues to sustain his creation, and Scripture tells us that the Holy Spirit actively restrains evil in the world. Thus, some significant vestiges of creation's goodness still persist. All parts of creation, from art to science to law and politics, merit our attention and our engagement. Nothing is irredeemably corrupt. Political Science, for example, enables Christians to study politics as the proper and effective use of power—as part of God's gifting of his creation, despite the distorted ends for which humans have often used it. As Christians, our task is not to avoid certain subjects for fear of contamination, but to engage them as part of God's blessings on his creation.

2. The "hermeneutics of suspicion"

Because of the Fall, however, Christians must approach academic life with a healthy dose of skepticism. If the doctrine of the Fall teaches us anything, it's that human beings can be selfish, corrupt, mistaken, and self-deluded—even when they are trying to do good. Christians call this phenomenon human depravity, and it affects scholarship in two important ways. First, because of our understanding of human nature, we would do well to apply what one scholar called a "hermeneutics of suspicion" to our studies. This rather ominous phrase simply means that we recognize that all humans have particular biases and want to be correct. Thus, intentionally or not, their interpretation of the evidence can be distorted by that desire. So as Christians we should approach any truth claim with both generosity *and* suspicion—whether that truth claim comes from Sigmund Freud or Billy Graham.

> *As Christians we should approach any truth claim with both generosity and suspicion—whether that truth claim comes from Sigmund Freud or Billy Graham.*

When I was growing up, for example, I learned from some Christian leaders that America was founded as a Christian nation. Later I read the primary documents for myself and discovered that a variety of secular and Christian influences contributed to the founding of America. The Christians who advocated the notion of America's Christian origins were not bad people; they simply allowed their good intentions to color their approach to history. The same dynamic occurs, to a greater or lesser extent, in all disciplines. Like speculators who rush in to buy Florida real estate, convinced that the boom market will never end, scholars throughout history have made breathless assertions about the "indisputable truth" of their findings, only to be proven wrong later. We need to approach any subject, therefore, with a healthy sense of skepticism.

Second, as fallen humans, we need to apply that same suspicion to ourselves. One of the most valuable qualities that Christian education can instill is a sense of intellectual humility—the ability to say, "I might be wrong about this." An awareness of our own fallenness and capacity for self-delusion enables us to learn from others and function as teachable members of a college community. The Fall teaches us to be wary of truth claims, but also to recognize our own need to be modest in our assertions and to learn from others. A Bible professor, for example, may not be infallible; but his years of study of ancient culture and languages means that his insights are worth considering when he challenges my assumptions about Genesis. The psychology professor whose ideas are new to me should prompt not defensiveness but curiosity—and then a generous, teachable skepticism.

3. The Fall necessitates careful study of the world.

For the Christian, one of the purposes of education is to help us understand the subtle, complex, and at times systemic effects of the Fall not just on individuals but on our world. Sin has a way of working its way into the very systems and structures of our lives and indeed entire societies. It has a pernicious tendency to make the abnormal and the monstrous seem normal, and that can make understanding the world a complicated task requiring careful study. Consider, for example, the following letter sent by a businessman to his boss concerning a shortage of muffles and ovens:

At this time three double-muffle ovens are in operation, with a capacity of 250 per day. Furthermore, currently under construction are five triple-muffle ovens with a daily capacity of 800. Today and in the next few days, two eight-muffle ovens, each with a daily capacity of 800, will come on consignment, redirected from Mogilew. Mr. K said that this number of muffles is not yet sufficient; we should deliver more ovens as quickly as possible.

This letter seems to describe the ordinary stuff of business—buying and selling products, keeping up with demand, etc. Except that in this particular example, the businessman is an employee of the German industrial firm *Topf und Sohne* and the "products" are crematory ovens for Auschwitz death camp. The "capacity" refers to the number of human beings that can be cremated per day! This normalizing of evil all seems rather monstrous to us today, but if you had been a German worker in the 1940s and had grown up in a society steeped in German racial doctrines and the importance of obeying authority, would you have recognized it as such? Many German Christians did not.

What enables us to recognize the situation above as evil is a Christian worldview that considers the elimination of whole races as evil, and more importantly the benefit of historical perspective. But we do not have historical perspective on our own society, or enough social distance to recognize the subtle ways that sin infiltrates our own system of life. For example, as Christians who believe that all people are made in God's image, we believe that all human beings should have an equal opportunity for success in life. But we live in a society in which the playing field is often severely slanted. I attended high school in the western suburbs of Chicago, where about 75% of young people earned their high school diploma. In inner-city Detroit, 25% of young people graduate from high school. Is that discrepancy because suburban Chicago has smarter people than Detroit? Of course not. Rather, it stems in part from an American educational system in which the benefits and services flow toward those communities with greater economic resources.

Or consider the global economic structures that shape our lives. In the 1800s, northern Christians in the U.S. condemned slavery in the South. But they also bought the cotton products that made slave labor in the South such a profitable enterprise. Once again, with the advantage of history, we can recognize the northerners' culpability in the institution of slavery. But without a careful study of economics and sociology in modern society, we may fail to notice economic systems today that may encourage injustice in remote parts of the world. Does my purchase of Nike running shoes, for example, contribute to the exploitation of a worker in a sweatshop in Malaysia? That would hardly rank up there with producing ovens for Auschwitz, but it's

> *One purpose of Christian higher education is to develop the ability to recognize the complex effects of the Fall on creation. Condemning genocide is easy; understanding deep, subtle, and complex systemic evils is not.*

participation in a sinful system nonetheless—and it's often difficult to discern.

One of the key questions that a student at a Christian college must ask is, "How is the cultural arena that my major is preparing me for *not* the way it's supposed to be?" Answering that question, however, can be difficult when we swim in the same cultural waters that we are attempting to study. One purpose of Christian education, therefore, is to develop the ability to recognize the complex effects of the Fall on creation. Condemning genocide is relatively easy; understanding deep, subtle, and complex systemic evils is not. Doing so requires an understanding of history, theology, social sciences, and other subjects. And it requires a thorough knowledge of your own major in light of a Christian worldview.

4. The Fall requires flexibility.

As with human society in general, college life demonstrates an intermingling of the good of creation with the corruption of the Fall. Take a typical college soccer game, for example. As we have seen, play is rooted in the doctrine of creation. A soccer game allows human beings to "image" God by delighting in creation, and it applies the cultural mandate by developing the human impulse to play into a particular structure where athletic creativity and cooperation can thrive. Moreover, friendly athletic competition can contribute to human community. Yet the athletic beauty of a soccer game this side of heaven comes accompanied by the baggage of the Fall. Dazzling saves are matched by slide tackles from behind and taunting of opponents. Spectators cheer their team—until the first questionable call, after which the cheers turn into angry berating of the referees.

Other aspects of college life demonstrate the same mixture of goodness and fallenness. A new computer game provides fun and collegiality in the dorm. But some students are so entranced by the game that they waste hours on it and neglect their studies and sleep. And, of course, a significant number of college students, on both secular and Christian campuses, corrupt the intrinsic good of academic learning by plagiarizing papers from the internet or cheating on exams. Once again, the evil—cheating—attaches itself like a parasite to the prior good of Christian learning. All of these areas, however, are peripheral to the main focus of this book—the college classroom. So how does the Fall affect academics in particular? Actually, the answer to that question is fairly complicated.

Christians generally agree that sin corrupts not just the human will and emotions but also the mind. The question is to what extent. In other words, how does the Fall affect the average person's ability to think and to understand the world correctly? Or to put it bluntly, does your chemistry textbook bear the marks of the Fall? It's a question that Christian theologians have debated for centuries, and one that bears directly on our lives at a Christian college.

Some have believed that non-Christian thinkers are so darkened in their understanding that they cannot think or write (or paint or compose) correctly. Academic disciplines depend on prior assumptions, and in some disciplines those assumptions are biased against supernaturalism. For example, Richard Lewontin, a Harvard biologist, once confessed his guiding faith commitment in scientific materialism:

> We have a prior commitment to materialism. It is not that the methods and institutions of science somehow compel us to

accept a material explanation of the phenomenal world, but on the contrary, that we are forced by our *a priori* adherence to material causes to create an apparatus of investigation and a set of concepts that produce material explanations, no matter how counterintuitive, no matter how mystifying to the uninitiated. Moreover, that materialism is absolute, for we cannot allow a Divine Foot in the door.

Lewontin's materialistic bias is one that many modern scientists share, though rarely do they acknowledge their assumptions as honestly as he does. Richard Dawkins, for example, has achieved celebrity status by championing naturalistic evolution as the only reasonable position for modern people to hold.

Even the arts bear the heavy imprint of the Fall. A few years ago Aliza Shvarts, an art student at Yale University, presented a rather unusual senior project: She claimed to have artificially inseminated herself with sperm, then "performed" what she called "repeated self-induced miscarriages." Her purpose, she said, was to raise questions about society and the body, namely the stigma that society attaches to the term "miscarriage." To many, however, especially in the Christian community, her exhibit was simply evidence of the hopelessly corrupt nature of modern art.

Faced with countless examples of the Fall's effects on culture, Christians often take an oppositional stance toward science and

> *The doctrine of common grace provides an important foundation for education.*

art. But our task is more complicated than that, since often unbe-lievers have insights from which we need to learn. As noted earlier, the doctrine of common grace provides an important foundation for education. John Calvin was as firm a believer in human depravity as any Christian in history. But even Calvin acknowledged that the unbeliever can discover truths about God's creation.

It would be easy, of course, simply to dismiss Richard Dawkins, Charles Darwin, or Sigmund Freud as unredeemable opponents of Christianity, or to use Ms. Shvart's aborted fetuses as an excuse to condemn modern art altogether. But doing so would be to shirk our duty to understand all of God's creation and deprive ourselves of possible insights. In any academic discipline, we should ask ques-tions such as: To what extent does this subject rely on unspoken as-sumptions? Which of those assumptions overlap with a Christian worldview? How does common grace affect this subject? The writer of the chemistry textbook, after all, may believe that all of life can be reduced to chemical processes. But that does not prevent the Christian from learning about ionic and covalent bonds from the book nonetheless.

Simply put, the Fall affects the various subjects that we study in different ways. What the Christian student needs above all, there-fore, is *flexibility* in approaching human thought and culture. Let me explain:

Andy Crouch's book *Culture Making: Recovering Our Creative Calling* contains an insightful chapter entitled "Gestures and Postures." Human beings make a variety of bodily gestures in the course of a day, and over time gestures that are repeated develop postures. A posture is the body's default position, the one that we take when we aren't paying attention to it. My daughter, for example, is a ballet dancer, and her countless hours in the studio have resulted in a light, graceful walking gait. My wife's grandfather, a farmer, spent so many years picking vegetables that when I met him as an old man, his back was permanently inclined at an angle.

Crouch observes that in the cultural realm too, gestures can become postures—a phenomenon demonstrate in history by American Christians. A century ago, conservative Christians so frequently condemned worldly ideas and behaviors that their gesture became an instinctive posture of *condemnation* toward secular culture and ideas. These conservatives were followed by a generation of Christians in the mid-twentieth century who rejected the separatism of their parents. They sought instead to *critique* culture by analyzing cultural products from a Christian worldview perspective.

In the 1960s and 1970s, evangelicals launched the Christian youth culture and "CCM," or contemporary Christian music. They sought to *copy* culture by importing the forms of rock music and pop culture into the safe bubble of the Christian subculture. For many of us today, the self-consciously Christian and derivative nature of CCM bands, with their T-shirts and Christian Woodstocks, may seem a bit cheesy. A common posture for Christians today, Crouch observes, is cultural *consumption* when it comes to music, books, films, or technology. That is, they uncritically watch films, surf the web, or maintain their Facebook page with little attention to how such behaviors may be subtly affecting them or their communities.

Crouch's insights apply to academic life as well. All of these gestures are potentially appropriate; it just depends on the subject. Take

> *The college classroom will be characterized by critique—understood not simply as "criticism" but rather the attempt to understand and analyze a subject in its proper context.*

the study of film, for example. One of the primary goals of Christian education is to produce mature, thinking students who can evaluate the world around them from a Christian perspective. And that applies to the films we watch. But only when doing so is appropriate. You could, of course, apply *critique* to the *Shrek* films by analyzing them as a commentary on the "princess" motif in Western literature and a parody of modern culture's preoccupation with external physical appearance. But if you do, you'll probably just annoy those around you who are busy laughing at the earthy jokes and witty dialogue. It's probably best just to sit back and enjoy—or *consume*—*Shrek* as a funny film.

Other films, such as *The Social Network*, require more of a combination of both consumption and critique. Its scenes depicting Harvard student life and sharp dialogues are very entertaining, but the film also raises deep questions about technology and human community that merit critique and analysis from a Christian perspective. Still others, such as *Hotel Rwanda*, may be disturbing to watch, but merit our attention because of the disturbing subjects for moral reflection that they raise. And finally, there are films that simply deserve *condemnation* as worthy of neither entertainment nor reflection.

The same variability of approaches applies to other academic subjects as well. The college classroom is most often associated with *critique*—understood not simply as "criticism" but rather the attempt to understand and analyze a subject in its proper context. But many intellectual and cultural products also are meant to be consumed, not just analyzed. We can take critique too far if we miss the enjoyment of an eloquent poem, a beautiful painting, or even an elegant scientific theory. Shakespeare's plays merit critique and analysis, but we would also do well to *copy* them—that is, to have Shakespeare's marvelous feel for words and the rhythm of language leaven our own writing. Physics students should seek to understand and analyze Einstein's theories, but they should also emulate Einstein's ability to grasp the simple concept amid the complexities. Finally, in a world darkened by the Fall, Christians must retain *condemnation* as an option as well. For example, Hitler's *Mein Kampf* can be studied as a window into the culture of early-twentieth-century Germany, but ultimately its pernicious racial doctrines deserve our condemnation. In other words, it's often helpful to frame one's study of a subject around the guiding question: "What is the most appropriate gesture, or combination of gestures, to assume in relation to this particular subject or artifact?"

As Christian scholars, our approach to a subject must remain flexible and discerning depending on the nature of that subject and its connection to the Fall. It comes down to knowing when to condemn, when to copy, when to critique, and when to consume; and the answers are rarely straightforward. That's why ultimately Christian education depends on wisdom rather than a prescribed formula. It would be easier, of course, to adopt a single posture to govern our approach to academics. But that would also be shallower, and much less interesting. God calls us to study his world in all of its beauty and its fallenness. Doing so requires a robust approach to education and a nimbleness of mind to adopt different stances in different situations.

A Note on Sources

The most thorough recent treatment of the doctrine of the Fall is Cornelius Plantinga's *Not the Way It's Supposed to Be: A Breviary of Sin* (Eerdmans, 1995). Michael Wittmer's quote on the extensive effects of Adam's sin is found in his book *Heaven Is a Place on Earth: Why Everything You Do Matters to God* (Zondervan, 2004), 173. C. S. Lewis is quoted in Cornelius Plantinga's *Engaging God's World* (Eerdmans, 2002), 53. The *Topf und Sohne* letter can be found online at the Holocaust History Project (http://www.holocaust-history.org/). Richard Lewontin is quoted in Plantinga, 68. Andy Crouch's discussion of gestures and postures is found in *Culture Making* (InterVarsity, 2008), chapter 5. All Scripture citations are from the New International Version.

Questions for Reflection and Discussion

1. Why are "systemic" evils often so difficult to detect and to combat?

2. What practices of modern Christians do you think Christians a century from now will criticize? Give examples.

3. What would be a specific example of how your own major is impacted by the Fall?

4. Which posture toward culture has been the most common in your own background?

5. How does one determine which posture to adopt in a particular academic or cultural setting?

5 BROADCASTING MOZART

The Doctrine of Redemption

So far we have explored two main acts of the Christian story and their implications for college: All things were created good by God, and all things have been marred by the Fall. Here's part three of the story: God in Christ is working to redeem all of his creation and restore it to the way it was supposed to be. That doesn't necessarily mean that all people will be redeemed. Humans have free will, and therefore the ability to reject God. But the rest of creation doesn't have a choice in the matter. According to the Bible, it will be restored to its original goodness, and God's people will play an important role in that restoration.

As with the doctrine of the Fall, many of us grow up hearing so much about the notion of redemption that it becomes commonplace to us. Redemption, I learned when I was younger, basically meant "accepting Jesus into your heart so you can go to heaven." While that's an important part of the story, there's much more to it. The doctrine of redemption is marvelous in its complexity and its implications for all of creation—and ultimately for our understanding of a college education. Indeed, one could argue that our notion of a college education will be as large or as small as our understanding of redemption. A weak notion of redemption has sometimes led

Christians to treat college as simply a training session for evangelism or missions; or as training for a "secular" career to pay the bills for those Christians who are involved in "real" ministry. Conversely, if we have a broad understanding of redemption, college becomes rich with virtually endless possibilities. This chapter will briefly sketch a robust biblical doctrine of redemption, then explore its implications for Christian education.

We'll begin by returning to the story of the Fall in Genesis 3. Immediately after Adam and Eve receive the penalty for their disobedience (and creation in general is cursed), God sets out fixing things by making "garments of skin" to clothe their nakedness. By chapter twelve, God has selected one person in particular, Abraham, to establish a beachhead of redemption for the human race. God tells Abraham: "All peoples on earth will be blessed through you" (12:3). In other words, Abraham's descendants, the nation of Israel, are intended to be a model of a human society that functions the way things were supposed to be. The Israelites had a term for this: *shalom*, which we often translate as "peace," but which, as Cornelius Plantinga explains, meant a lot more to the Israelites than just an absence of conflict: "In the Bible, shalom means universal flourishing, wholeness, and delight—a rich state of affairs in which natural needs are satisfied and natural gifts fruitfully employed, all under the arch of God's love."

The Old Testament prophets hinted at this state of *shalom* that would encompass both the human and natural worlds. Isaiah exclaimed, "The desert and the parched land will be glad; the wilderness will rejoice and blossom" (35:1). Later he says, "They will build houses and dwell in them; they will plant vineyards and eat their fruit. . . . The wolf and the lamb will feed together, and the lion will eat straw like the ox" (65:21, 25). Someday, the prophets proclaimed, all creation will be made right and things will once again be the way God created them to be.

The incarnation of Jesus Christ, of course, is the key act in the biblical drama of redemption. In the person of Jesus, God takes on human form, accepts the penalty for sin on the cross, and conquers Satan and death through the resurrection. Christ establishes his Church, a people who will be the key agents in extending Christ's victory over sin to the entire creation. Paul sums up the cosmic significance of Christ's work in his letter to the Colossians: "God was pleased to have all his fullness dwell in him, and through him to reconcile to himself all things, whether things on earth or things in heaven, by making peace through his blood, shed on the cross" (1:19-20).

The redemption story culminates in John's vision of a new heaven and new earth in the book of Revelation. He writes: "I saw the Holy City, the new Jerusalem, coming down out of heaven from God, prepared as a bride beautifully dressed for her husband. And I heard a loud voice from the throne saying, 'Now the dwelling of God is with men, and he will live with them. . . . There will be no more death or mourning or crying or pain, for the old order of things has passed away'" (21:2-4). Between Christ's victory over death on the cross and this

> *We as Christians live "between the times," extending the effects of redemption and nudging creation closer to its final consummation in Christ.*

final consummation foretold by John, we as Christians live "between the times," extending the effects of redemption and nudging creation closer to its final consummation in Christ.

So what does all of this mean for our daily lives here on earth? To understand that, it can be helpful to consider what Jesus meant when he talked about the "Kingdom of God." American Christians often have misinterpreted this phrase in one of two ways. First, they take Jesus' remark that "the Kingdom of God is within you" to mean that the Kingdom of God is primarily a matter of having one's inward state redeemed and focused on God. Second, Christians sometimes equate the Kingdom of God solely with the future state of heaven, and thus look at the present life as just some sort of waiting stage before real life begins. As the traditional Negro spiritual puts it: "This world is not my home, I'm just a passin' through." A more biblical way of thinking about the Kingdom of God, however, is as a *condition* rather than a location. That is, when Jesus talks about the Kingdom of God, he is referring to the active exercise of God's kingly office, which is partially in place in creation now but which will ultimately extend to all of creation, just as it did at the beginning of time.

Albert Wolters employs a helpful analogy to communicate this point: On June 6, 1944, in an event known as D-Day, the armies of the U.S. and Great Britain established a beachhead in Nazi-occupied northern France. This crucial victory paved the way for the eventual re-conquest of all of Western Europe from the control of Germany. But the final victory did not come until the fall of Berlin on May 8, 1945. As Christians, we can think of Christ's death and resurrection as our D-Day, providing the key turning point in the war against Satan and evil. But the ultimate victory will not come until Christ's

Second Coming. In the meantime, we are engaged in multiple ways in extending the restoration of Christ's rule throughout creation.

Here's a way to visualize the concept: As Christians, we sometimes envision our lives as divided into "sacred" and "secular" compartments, like this:

church family personal life	**the "sacred," Kingdom of God**
politics business art school sports entertainment	**the "secular," Kingdom of the World**

Thus, when we go to church or relate to others we are engaging in "Christian" life, but when we watch a film or go to work, we are just engaging in "normal life."

In a proper understanding of the world and God's intention for it, however, there is no such thing as just normal life. Every part of creation is involved in the struggle to extend Christ's reign over all of his creation. Thus, we can visualize the above scenario a better way:

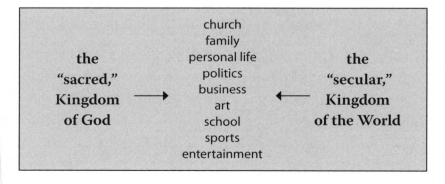

When we apply our calling as Christians to our careers in business or to the political process, God's reign is extended more completely over creation.

Obviously, the implications of this view of redemption for college are vast. In fact, most Christian colleges probably would claim that their main purpose is to equip students to function as effective agents of redemption throughout all of creation. Here are three particular ways that redemption relates to education.

1. Redeeming your academic discipline

Most specifically, we can look at our academic subjects themselves as objects of redemption. Let me explain:

Christians sometimes remark that "only people are eternal." But that's not necessarily the case. In *Culture Making*, Andy Crouch points out the theological implications of John's vision of the Heavenly City in Revelation, which we discussed in chapter three. The city, as described by John, is full of cultural artifacts that have been refined and perfected. The city walls consist of jewels—natural artifacts that have been refined by human culture. The city itself, the prophet Isaiah foretells in chapter 60, will be filled with "the glory of the nations." In Isaiah's prophetic vision, not just "Christian" stuff but the best products of human culture— the camels of desert tribes, the swift ships of Tarshish, the beautifully hewn timbers of Lebanon—make a grand processional to the Heavenly City. The reader can almost picture a Disneyworld ride in which every nation displays an idealized form of its most characteristic product, except that in this case the products are real, not plastic or paper maché.

In a certain sense, then, not just people but *things* have eternal value. As theologian Richard Mouw says, "The final vision of the city is one filled . . . not just with redeemed persons from every cultural background, but with redeemed human culture too." But the key word there is *redeemed*. Human culture must be redeemed and refined before it is suitable for eternity. Such an understanding can revolutionize our approach to college, since much of college life consists of studying and producing cultural goods. A good question to ask ourselves, therefore, when dealing with any cultural product in college is, "What would it take for this object, or subject of study, to make it into the Heavenly City?"

> *Most Christian colleges probably would argue that their main purpose is to equip students to function as effective agents of redemption throughout all of creation.*

What would it mean to "redeem" your subject of study in college? How about as an art major? Let's return to an example from the previous chapter, Aliza Shvarts, the Yale art student who created "art" from miscarriages. Naturally, the Christian artist would want to share the gospel with Shvarts (probably in a more sophisticated manner than quoting John 3:16). But the Christian artist also seeks to "redeem" the medium of art itself, to make it the way it was supposed to be and suitable for the Heavenly City. We do so by creating artwork that expresses the human condition in all its beauty, complexity, and at times perhaps even ugliness. That doesn't mean that redeemed art must depict Mary and the baby Jesus or cozy cottages nestled beside babbling brooks. It may not convey a clear subject at all. Makoto Fujimura, a Christian artist in New York City, creates visually stunning abstract art using minerals which he pulverizes into various pigments. One of his purposes is to "redeem" the medium of abstract art.

Redemption of this sort is more easily visualized in a hands-on major such as studio art. But what about a more abstract area of study such as history? At some point in your academic career you will not only learn about history but also *do* history yourself. And when you do, it will be helpful to ask questions such as: In what ways does the discipline of history bear the marks of the Fall? Have historians at times distorted their accounts or failed to tell the whole story? Have they even falsified their evidence or stolen material from other scholars? How can Christians "redeem" the study of history? That is, how can we produce historical scholarship that is rich, profound, accurate, and engaging? If we assume that real events will occur in the Heavenly City, then it's likely that there will be historians there to record and interpret those events. How are you as a student preparing yourself to write the kind of history—or compose poetry, or conduct scientific experiments—that will make it into eternity? Part of our task as cultural beings is to

> *Part of our task as cultural beings is to redeem the cultural products that have been corrupted by the Fall, and college is a great place to begin doing that.*

redeem the cultural products that have been corrupted by the Fall, and college is a great place to begin doing that.

2. Redeeming the world through your discipline

For most students, the purpose of college is not necessarily to "redeem" their major but to have that major prepare them to live effectively in the world. This is the most obvious way that redemption applies to higher education. One can work on a car, fixing broken parts, tinkering with the engine, waxing the paint, and so on. But ultimately one needs to get behind the wheel, start the engine, and drive the car somewhere. In the same way, as Christians we can and should study our disciplines from a Christian perspective, and some students will be called to devote their lives to such a task. But most students will be called to drive their major somewhere—in other words, to use it to make a difference in the world. The art student will use his sculptures to bring beauty to corners of creation where it did not exist before. The English major will use her education to open the eyes of sixth-graders to the power of written prose.

Any Christian college that takes its mission seriously, therefore, will seek to prepare students to "change the world," as some of them put it. But how exactly does one do that? Actually, the notion of redeeming culture has been the subject of a good deal of discussion and disagreement among Christians. One approach, championed by Charles Colson, begins with the assumption that cultures are shaped primarily by *ideas*—in the case of modern culture, ideas such as materialism, moral relativism, and postmodernism. Our task as Christians, therefore, is to be active in the public square in championing a Christian worldview and working to change the dominant ideas and institutions of society. Other Christians downplay the importance of worldviews and ideas, focusing instead on obeying Christ's teachings to minister to the poor and helpless in society and working to establish social justice in the U.S. and abroad. Jesus was not a "cultural warrior," they argue, but devoted his life to ministering to the outcasts of society. His followers are called to do the same. Others, such as Andy Crouch, meanwhile, advocate that Christians should engage in "culture making," and that the best way to change culture is not by combating it but by making new and better cultural goods. The iPod, after all, did not have to search and destroy the Sony Walkman; it was simply a better product.

The sociologist James Davison Hunter has criticized such attempts to change culture as naïve and misguided. Cultures, Hunter argues, change slowly and imperceptibly over centuries, and they do so through the influence of cultural elites and institutions—not through the work of ordinary people arguing their ideas, helping the poor, or making culture. The best that Christians can hope for, according to Hunter, is to exercise a "faithful presence" in society, as the Israelites did as exiles in Babylon, and not worry about trying to change the culture.

Obviously this debate is more complex than I am describing here, and advocates on all sides have some basis in Scripture. Perhaps a helpful way to envision our cultural task is to consider the example of Jesus. When we look at how Christ interacted with his world, several cultural approaches emerge:

- **Proclamation**: At times Jesus publically proclaimed the Good News of the Kingdom and his role in it. As he announced in the synagogue in Nazareth, "The Spirit of the Lord is upon me, because he has anointed me to preach good news to the poor. . . ."

- **Ministry to the poor**: Jesus spent much of his time meeting the physical needs of "the least of these" in society through healing the sick, feeding the hungry, and other acts of compassion.

- **Crossing cultural barriers**: In his conversation with the Samaritan woman and his dinner at the home of the tax collector, Jesus crossed the cultural barriers of Jewish society by associating with people considered "unacceptable" by the religious leaders of his day.

- **Withdrawal**: At times Jesus withdrew from the crowds to focus on his own relationship with God or to mentor his inner circle of disciples.

- **Active resistance**: At times Jesus intentionally and aggressively opposed the cultural system of his day, such as when he healed people on the Sabbath and drove the money-changers out of the temple.

- **Passive non-resistance**: In contrast to his aggressive resistance, Jesus could be surprisingly passive in his response to culture— most notably during his trial and crucifixion in which he offered no reply or resistance to his accusers.

What is clear from the example of Jesus, therefore, is that no single approach to interacting with culture is sufficient. Christians must be adept at a variety of ways of acting in the world, and know when each approach is appropriate. That is why ultimately Christian colleges equip students not just with knowledge or skills, but with *wisdom*. Christians must excel in a wide variety of areas and have a depth of insight about their world to understand what stance is most appropriate at a given time.

In sum, Christians are called to be active in culture in a variety of ways, and in doing that we can let God worry about whether our particular efforts "change the world" on a global scale. And fortunately there are enough different types of Christians with unique gifts and interests to fulfill the calling to champion a Christian worldview in the public square, to combat global injustice, to minister to the poor, to make culture, and to fulfill a host of other redemptive tasks. Gabe Lyons describes Christians as "restorers" who, like a builder remodeling a beautiful but dilapidated mansion, are engaged in making the world what God intended it to be. He writes: "Instead of waiting for God to unveil the new heaven and the new earth, the rest of us can give the world a taste of what God's kingdom is all about—building up, repairing brokenness, showing mercy, reinstating hope, and generally adding value. In this expanded model, everyone plays an essential role."

> *Just as a carpenter needs training in order to remodel the house, so Christians need education in the complex cultural tasks of modern society if they are to be effective restorers of God's creation.*

But just as a carpenter needs training in order to remodel the house, so Christians need education in the complex cultural tasks of modern society if they are to be effective restorers of God's creation. As we saw in the previous chapter, the effects of the Fall are often complex; therefore, the work of restoration requires rigorous study and intelligent action. The benefit of historical perspective can help one to perceive systemic evils such as Naziism. But if you were a German Christian in the 1940s, how would you go about *fixing* such an institutional evil or alleviating the plight of the Jews? Doing so is no simple task. Academic study can help us become aware of the subtle and systemic effects of the Fall on human society. But recognizing that young people in suburban Chicago graduate from high school at a higher rate than young people in inner-city Detroit is one thing; *changing* it is another. It requires an understanding of sociology and how social structures change, as well as politics, economics, and psychology. It will probably help to study history to learn from the attempts of social reformers in the past. In all of these ways, college education equips us to redeem parts of creation more strategically and effectively.

Understanding our redemptive calling, therefore, makes college come alive in a whole new way. A major in engineering doesn't just prepare you for a career and a decent salary (though if you do your work well that is a probable byproduct). It equips you to advance the work of restoration as an engineer—perhaps by developing clean water technology that counteracts the effects of the Fall on our natural resources. A course in microeconomics doesn't just prepare you for a future job in business; it's one small part of the "engine" that will drive you into parts of the world that require an understanding of economic behavior in order to improve them. A degree in law may equip you to advance justice in one small corner of God's kingdom. If we trace the connections, we can find all sorts of particular ways that our college studies prepare us to contribute to God's redemptive work in the world.

3. Intelligent evangelism

Of course, there is one more important way that Christians advance Christ's reign in creation: by telling others about Jesus. As a recent *Christianity Today* editorial put it, the world's greatest social need is for people to be reconciled to God spiritually. In a world in which millions of people do not believe in Christ, evangelism remains one of our primary redemptive tasks. I have waited to raise this point, however, because historically evangelical Christians have been quick to focus on "saving souls," often to the exclusion of other concerns. When that happens, evangelism becomes forced, artificial, and unconvincing, if not downright awkward. But when Christians are actively and effectively engaged in the task of restoration in all parts of culture, then the conditions are favorable for evangelism. As theologian Lesslie Newbigin observed: "Where the church is faithful to the Lord, *there* the powers of the Kingdom are present and people begin to ask the questions to which the Gospel is the answer."

Or, to put it another way—we as Christians are called to excellence in our personal lives, in our careers, and in every other area of life. When we do that, the merits of the gospel naturally emerge. As Charles Murray once observed concerning the great Christian composer, J. S. Bach: "When human beings are functioning at the heights of human capacity, it is a good idea to begin by assuming that they are doing something right. Johann Sebastian Bach does not need to explain himself; the beauty and excellence of his music itself make a case that his way of looking at the universe needs to be taken seriously." That doesn't mean that one's vocation is simply a platform for evangelism, as if the only purpose for writing great music is to witness to other musicians. Such an argument would undermine the whole notion that our work as Christians is valuable in its own right.

But *when* verbal proclamation is necessary and appropriate, we as Christians need to do so intelligently. That's because, for most of us who graduate from college, sharing our faith will occur in the course of our lives as "white-collar" professionals among society's educated class. Thus it will probably require more intellectual sophistication than it did for Christians in previous generations. When I was a Christian college student, I took a course entitled "Personal Evangelism." In it we learned evangelistic techniques such as the Romans Road, in which the Christian led the non-believer through a series of passages in the book of Romans such as Romans 3:23—"For all have sinned and have fallen short of the glory of God." It seems that quarterback Tim Tebow took my Personal Evangelism class, or something like it. A few years ago, he made headlines when he appeared in the college football national championship game sporting "John 3:16" in bright white characters on his black eye-glare patches.

The Romans Road and John 3:16 eye-patch methods may be effective, but they depend on a very

> *A Christian college education will help you to become the kind of empathetic, insightful, and interesting person with whom a modern unbeliever with sincere questions about Christianity would feel comfortable talking.*

big assumption—that the person being evangelized shares my belief that the Bible is the Word of God and speaks with unique authority about spiritual matters. But as cultural observers will attest, a paradigm shift concerning the notion of truth has occurred in recent decades. For many modern Americans, what constitutes "truth" is defined individually or in communities; thus multiple versions of truth can exist with little impact on each other. Moreover, the typical secular American would likely view Christianity as simply one of many ways of getting in touch with spiritual forces. What good does it do, therefore, for a Christian to emblazon "John 3:16" on his eye-patches if most Americans view the Bible as just one of many inspiring books, along with the Koran and the Book of Mormon?

Effective evangelism today requires that we understand the assumptions that lie beneath the thinking of modern secular people and the kinds of questions they are asking. You may have to discuss the nature of truth and the problem of evil with your fellow engineer before you can get to John 3:16. You may begin with a discussion of a recent film or book that illustrates theological concepts. And for such conversations, a Christian college education can be extremely useful. You will learn logic and basic principles of evidence in a Philosophy course; how the modern worldview has been shaped in Western or World Civilization; how to speak and write persuasively in Composition or Oral Communication; how to understand and empathize with the modern mentality as expressed in modern art and music; how the Bible speaks to the modern condition in Theology class. In short, a Christian college education will help you become the kind of empathetic, insightful, and interesting person with whom a modern unbeliever with sincere questions about Christianity would feel comfortable talking. You'll prepare yourself not just to proclaim the gospel, but to do so in ways that are effective in modern culture.

In the 1994 film *Shawshank Redemption*, a wealthy businessman, played by Tim Robbins, has been wrongfully convicted of a crime and finds himself in the Massachusetts state penitentiary. The prison is controlled by a corrupt warden and his henchmen, who abuse the prisoners and siphon funds meant for the convicts into their own pockets. Because of his business skills, Robbins works in the prison's main office. One day he is filing old musical albums and comes across a recording of a Mozart opera. Robbins' eyes light up as he gets an idea. He locks himself in the office, puts the record on the record player, and broadcasts the music through the P.A. system throughout the entire prison grounds. As the camera pans across the prison yard, we see the dirty, demoralized prisoners momentarily entranced by the beauty of Mozart's aria flowing through the air. Recounts Morgan Freeman, Robbins' fellow prisoner: "I have no idea to this day what those two Italian ladies were singing about . . . . It was like some beautiful bird flapped into our drab cage and made those walls dissolve away. And for the briefest of moments, every last man at Shawshank felt free."

We can think of our work of redemption as "broadcasting Mozart" into a fallen world. Our college education prepares us for a vocation that will help to infuse truth, love, beauty, and order into a world that is marred by oppression, ugliness, and disorder. But we can carry the analogy further. Tim Robbins was powerless to change the prison system. A prison revolt inspired by a Mozart aria would have been good drama but not very realistic. Eventually the prison

> *We can think of our work of redemption as "broadcasting Mozart" into a fallen world. Our college education prepares us to inject truth, love, beauty, and order into a world that is marred by injustice, ugliness, and drudgery.*

guards break into his office, destroy the Mozart record, throw Robbins into solitary confinement, and the prison reverts to the status quo. Thus, Robbins' contribution was to make the conditions more bearable for his fellow prisoners and to point them to a better world beyond the prison walls.

But if Robbins had wielded more power in the penitentiary—for example, as a prison guard, or even the warden—then merely providing beautiful music for the prisoners would have been inadequate. We would expect him to work to correct the abuses and injustices of the prison complex. Money intended for the penitentiary would purchase new clothes for the prisoners, not supplement the warden's private bank account. Guards who abused prisoners would be punished. Prisoners would be rehabilitated, not just punished. In other words, Robbins' "redemptive" work would have changed if his cultural location and power had been different.

As Christians, therefore, we need to have the wisdom to discern at what points in our culture we have the power, and the duty, to change the system itself. For some, our main redemptive calling may be to use our careers and talents to "broadcast Mozart" into the world and to evangelize those within the system—in other words, to exercise a "faithful presence" in our particular sphere of creation. Others will be called to change the system itself—to practice a "faithful resistance," if you will, to the status quo. Often, of course, it will be a combination of both. In each case, a college education is crucial and valuable. It not only prepares us for a career, but more importantly it equips us to play a role in restoring God's creation to the way it was supposed to be.

A Note on Sources

The concept of *shalom* is discussed in Cornelius Plantinga's *Engaging God's World* (Eerdmans, 2002), 14-15. Albert Wolters's D-Day analogy and the sacred/secular diagram are found in his book *Creation Regained* (Eerdmans, 1985), 66-70. Richard Mouw is quoted in Andy Crouch's discussion of the Heavenly City in *Making Culture* (InterVarsity, 2008), 163-174. Gabe Lyons's remark about "restorers" is in his book *The Next Christians* (Doubleday, 2010), 60. Lesslie Newbigin is quoted in Lyons, 195. Charles Murray's remark concerning J. S. Bach is from "For God's Eye: The Surprising Role of Christianity in Cultural Achievement," in *The American Enterprise* (October/November, 2003). The *Christianity Today* editorial "The Greatest Social Need" was published in January 2009.

In addition to the sources cited above, two important works on Christians' cultural calling are Charles Colson's *How Shall We Now Live* (Tyndale, 1999) and James Davison Hunter's *To Change the World* (Oxford, 2010).

Questions for Reflection and Discussion

1. How would your particular community function differently if *shalom* were more present there?

2. Why do you think that Christ has allowed so much time to pass between his first coming and his second coming?

3. What is one way that your own particular course of study stands in need of redemption?

4. Do you anticipate your particular calling in life to be "broadcasting Mozart" into the prison or changing the prison system itself? Explain.

5. How would you approach college differently if you envisioned it as a preparation for a life of "restoration"?

6. What is a recent book or film that you have encountered that would enable you to more effectively communicate the gospel to a non-Christian?

6 INTEGRATING FAITH AND LEARNING

A Basic Introduction

THE preceding chapters articulated the basic elements of a Christian worldview, summarized in the concepts of Creation, Fall, and Redemption. But what does this Christian worldview have to do with the actual academic process? Isn't algebra simply algebra, whether one is a Christian or not? It's time to explore more specifically how Christianity relates to the nuts and bolts of coursework at a Christian college. This chapter, therefore, will explain the concept known as "integration of faith and learning," then lay out some ways that Christians attempt to connect their Christian faith to their particular disciplines.

We'll begin, however, by discussing some common misconceptions of what it means to integrate faith and learning. First, integration is not simply a matter of encouraging personal relationships between professors and students. I once attended a faculty seminar on integration in which one professor described his pride at seeing a professor hug each of her students when they received their diplomas at graduation. He concluded, "If that's not the integration of faith and learning, I don't know what is." Actually, it's not. While of course the nurturing of close, mentoring relationships between professors and students is a good thing (and one of the most valuable qualities of a small Christian college), it is not what we typically mean by the integration of faith and learning. Such mentoring relationships could—and do—occur at secular and Christian institutions alike.

More than just the relationship between professor and student, the integration of faith and learning affects the actual classroom environment itself. Some Christians have interpreted this to mean that integration of faith and learning is synonymous with praying before class. While opening class with prayer is a good thing (students especially appreciate it on examination days), that's not what is meant by integration. If nothing in the professor's approach to the subject has anything to do with his or her Christian faith after the opening prayer, then a real, substantive integration of faith and learning has not occurred. The opening prayer may simply serve as a convenient tool to focus students' minds on the subject and remind them of their overall purpose in college.

This notion, that integration of faith and learning is primarily a matter of setting a spiritual atmosphere, stems from a shallow understanding of the relationship between Christian faith and academic inquiry. Some Christian educators have functioned as if Christianity and secular learning inhabit separate spheres. We learn spiritual and moral truths from the Bible, some would claim, and we learn about the physical world from academic disciplines. Thus, the task of a Christian college is to cultivate a pious atmosphere outside of class (through chapel, prayer groups, weekend retreats, and the like) while encouraging rigorous academic inquiry in the classroom. The problem with the "separate spheres" approach to learning is that it overlooks the fact that much of what we learn from science, psychology, and other disciplines has theological and moral implications. Furthermore, while not an academic textbook, the Bible nevertheless contains many implications about the makeup of the universe, the events and meaning of history, human nature, and other academic questions. To cite just one obvious example: The Christian who believes the biblical account of Jesus' resurrection would by necessity *dis*believe an archaeologist's claim to have discovered the bones of Jesus of Nazareth in an ancient Palestinian tomb.

The integration of faith and learning, therefore, goes beyond a pious atmosphere to the academic discipline itself. But even here, the concept can be misunderstood. Some Christians interpret integration primarily as a matter of including religious topics within one's area of study. I once attended a lecture by an English professor who explained that when teaching poetry she used passages from the Psalms as examples of various meters. That's fine, but it's not integration. We would not claim that a Christian carpenter who uses a Bible to prop up a table leg is integrating Christianity and furniture-making. Likewise, professors who insert religious material into their classes are not necessarily integrating faith and learning. Perceiving integration to be primarily a matter of studying "religious" topics allows

> *Simply put, integrating faith and learning means relating one's Christian worldview to an academic discipline.*

professors in, say, biology, to delegate the integration of faith and learning to people in theology while they concentrate on doing "real" science.

So if inadequate notions of the integration of faith and learning abound, what *do* we really mean by the term? To adequately understand integration, we need to refer back to the introductory chapter on Christian worldview. Simply put, integrating faith and learning means relating one's Christian worldview to an academic discipline. It is the ongoing process of understanding a subject in all of its complexity from a Christian perspective, and then to live out its moral and cultural implications. As such, integration involves not just an opening prayer, but the class lecture; and it applies to biology class as well as to Bible class. Scores of books have been written on this subject, but for our purposes we can think of the integration of faith and learning as occurring on three basic levels.

1. The motivational/relational level

The first level draws on some of our observations in the previous chapters: Our Christian faith motivates us to learn and apply a positive attitude toward the subject of study as a way to grow in our relationship with God. This is integration at its simplest level, but probably the most common level for the college student. For many non-Christians, the purpose of college is quite simple—to perform well, get good grades, and assemble an impressive resume for a career. In light of the doctrines of Creation, Fall, and Redemption, however, it should be clear that Christians have a higher purpose and deeper motivation for going to class. Each subject provides an opportunity to know God better, to more fully bear his image, and to become better able to participate in God's redemptive activity in the world.

Let me illustrate concerning the doctrine of creation: A few years ago my son was cleaning out the garage and came across some old spiral notebooks lying in the bottom of a box. They were my journals from my college days. Naturally, he was keenly interested in reading through them and learning more about his father during his developmental

> *A Christian worldview motivates us to learn and apply a positive attitude toward the subject of study. This is integration at its simplest level.*

years—though I was much more ambivalent about the prospect of my son reading my college journals. Imagine, however, that I had hired my neighbor's son to clean out the garage. He may have been amused at someone's college journals lying around in a garage, but he probably would have had little interest in reading through them.

My son's interest in the journals stems from his relationship to me. I'm his father, and the journals reveal things about his father that he wouldn't otherwise know. In the same way, the doctrine of Creation means that the universe is God's journal which reveals things about him that we would not learn in any other way. It's what theologians call God's "general revelation" revealing his characteristics and qualities, as distinct from the "special revelation" of the Bible.

Our basic motivation for learning biology, for example, stems from our relationship to God as the Creator of the wonderfully-complex life forms we study. Moreover, the doctrine of the *imago dei* implies that God equipped us with a natural curiosity about his creation, which we display when we study cells, algebra, or the French Revolution. And if that's not enough motivation, there's also the doctrine of redemption, which implies that fixing this broken world begins with a better understanding of the problems facing it. Integrating a Christian worldview and academics, therefore, begins with applying a positive attitude toward learning as a means of spiritual growth.

Such rhetoric may sound good in theory, but it can be more difficult to apply at the ground level. Having taught Western Civilization at 7:30 a.m., I know all too well that going to class does not always seem like reading the journals of God. So here are a couple of practical suggestions to help. First, if your instructor doesn't open class with prayer, it may help to say a silent prayer as a way to remind yourself of the larger purpose of class. It could be something as basic as the prayer "For Education" adapted from the *Book of Common Prayer*: "Almighty God, the fountain of all wisdom: Enlighten by your Holy Spirit those who teach and those who learn, that rejoicing in the knowledge of your truth, we may worship you and serve you better." Or one could pray at the beginning of class, "God, what is it in this class today that will enable me to know you better and love you more?" Such prayers serve to remind us that God is ultimately the source of truth and that every subject can help us to better worship and glorify him. That can be important when you find yourself sitting in a cold plastic chair at 7:30 in the morning.

Second, it may be helpful to work with other students to gain interest in and understanding of the subject. When I was in college, I enjoyed literature but was not particularly fond of chemistry. I had fellow students, however, who could get excited about learning chemistry. Discussing chemistry with them helped me not only to understand the subject better, but also to appreciate how the study of chemistry actually deepened their relationship with God. Thus it enabled me to have a more positive attitude toward the subject. Discussing course materials with others outside of class—during lunch or in the dormitory, for example—can increase your understanding and appreciation of the subject, even if it's outside your natural area of interest.

2. The intellectual/foundational level

Most Christians would acknowledge that Christian faith should result in a positive motivation toward learning. The integration of faith and learning, however, occurs not just at the attitudinal level but at the intellectual level as well. As explained in the introductory chapter, all academic inquiry stems from certain assumptions about the nature of reality, God's existence, human nature, and so on. Integrating faith and learning means that we consciously relate our Christian worldview to the area of study. What does psychology look like, for example, to the Christian who believes that human beings are creatures with a soul made in God's image rather than randomly evolved organisms? A course in psychology that integrates faith and learning at the intellectual level will tease out such implications of a Christian view of human nature.

But back to the chapter's opening question: Is there a "Christian" algebra? Not necessarily. When it comes to applying a Christian worldview at the intellectual level, some disciplines will tend to integrate faith and learning more explicitly than do others. There are

> *The more that a discipline deals with the nature of human beings, their cultural products, and the nature of ultimate reality the more explicit worldview questions become to the discourse.*

fewer areas in mathematics where a Christian worldview about the nuts and bolts of the subject is distinctive from a secular worldview than in, say, philosophy, a subject in which one's assumptions about the nature of reality are critical. We can thus think of integration as a continuum. Disciplines such as physics and chemistry focus almost exclusively on physical matter, and as such worldview questions do not typically intrude on the subject. When doing their jobs as chemists, Christians, atheists, Muslims, and others will generally agree about the makeup of molecules and their interactions, despite their different worldviews. Christian scholars may bring different motivations to their disciplines and reach different ethical conclusions from them, but in the actual scholarship itself, Christian faith will likely be more *implicit* than explicit.

The more that a discipline deals with the nature of human beings, their cultural products, and the nature of ultimate reality, however, the more explicitly worldview questions influence the discourse, since these are questions over which Christians and non-Christians are more likely to disagree. In psychology, for instance, one is never very far from basic worldview questions such as "Do human beings have a soul?" and "What is the basis of human motivation?" In other words, as we move from mathematics and natural science to the social sciences and the humanities, the more explicit one's worldview becomes, and thus more opportunity will exist for the integration of faith and learning, as the diagram below illustrates.

The Implicit/Explicit Continuum					
Implicit ——————————————————————— *Explicit*					
Mathematics	Natural Sciences	Social Sciences	History	Arts and Literature	Philosophy/ Theology

Even in the areas toward the left side of the continuum, however, the opportunity for integration never completely disappears. For example, in mathematics, scholars may differ over such foundational questions as, "Are numbers real or imagined?" "Is mathematical truth 'out there' to be discovered or is it invented in the mind of the mathematician?" The answers to these questions are inescapably linked to one's worldview. In the 1930s, Nazi scholars argued that there was a "German" mathematics and a "German" physics, as distinct from "Jewish" mathematics or physics; in other words, that mathematical and physical truth was not "out there" to be discovered but subject to the perspectives of one's race. Their assumptions about race and culture impacted their understanding even of the so-called "hard" sciences.

Recently some psychologists made headlines when they conducted what became known as the "invisible gorilla" experiment. They showed viewers a short video in which a group of people passed basketballs around, and they asked the viewers to count the number of passes made by the people in the white shirts. In the middle of the video, a man in a gorilla suit strolls into the middle of the action, faces the camera and thumps his chest, then leaves. Amazingly, over half of the viewers never saw the gorilla (including myself, the first time I watched it). The experiment demonstrated an important truth: Humans have a remarkable ability to see what they are looking for and not see what they don't look for. Often what scholars "see" in the data is shaped by their worldview assumptions and the questions that they bring to their scholarship. Integrating faith and learning at the foundational level, therefore, means allowing our Christian beliefs to pose interesting and provocative questions of our disciplines, and to notice things in our disciplines that others may not see.

3. The applied/ethical level

One of the potential dangers of a worldview approach to integration is that it can be misconstrued to imply that once we as Christians have "figured out" a discipline or critiqued it intellectually, our task is done. Christianity, however, is not a philosophy; it's a way of thinking *and acting* in the world. As cultural beings, our encounter with any new information or technique will ultimately prompt us to ask what use it will have in our actual lives. Karl Marx famously declared, "Up to now the purpose of philosophy has been to understand the world. But the purpose of philosophy is to *change* the world." As Christians, we do not have to accept all of Marx's philosophy to agree with him that as agents of redemption in the world we should seek to understand what difference a subject makes to the world around us.

The final way of integrating faith and learning, therefore, involves applying the knowledge from a particular discipline to the world in a way that furthers God's creative or redemptive purposes. In other words, it means using psychology to *help* people, not just understand them. Obviously, that involves doing, not just thinking. But before we can act, often we must wrestle with difficult academic questions. That is because when one moves from the subject itself to the *application* of that knowledge, one often

> *Integrating faith and learning, therefore, involves applying the knowledge from a particular discipline to the world in a way that furthers God's redemptive work.*

encounters a host of ethical questions that cannot be answered apart from worldviews. Einstein's famous equation $e=mc2$, for example, arouses little debate between Christian and non-Christian scholars. However, when one applies this scientific insight to society in terms of nuclear energy, all sorts of controversial questions arise. Should we develop nuclear bombs? If so, should they ever be used? What about nuclear power, which provides more energy with less pollution than fossil fuels but involves greater risk?

The same can be said for a seemingly "hard" discipline such as engineering. For example, engineers and builders may generally agree that a thinner, lighter window material could save thousands of dollars in material costs when constructing high-rise buildings. However, the cheaper windows may be more likely to blow out during a storm, endangering pedestrians below. At what point does using lower cost windows that increase the risk of human injury become immoral? The answer to this question depends on the relative value that one places on human beings and therefore human safety—in other words, on worldview questions. Or take the field of journalism: At what point does my obligation as a journalist to uncover the truth of a story conflict with my need to respect the privacy of vulnerable human beings who are made in God's image? Integrating faith and learning involves going from a subject itself to working out its practical and ethical consequences for individuals and cultures.

Asking the "integrative question"

The discussion above raises an important point: Wherever one's discipline falls on the continuum, one of the best ways to go about the actual task of integrating faith and learning is to ask what Christian scholar Harold Heie calls the "integrative question," that is, a question that cannot be answered without reference to both the discipline itself and a Christian worldview. Examples of such questions abound, and often what brings a subject alive to Christian college students is developing and wrestling with these sorts of questions. Here are just a few examples from across the implicit/explicit continuum:

> *Natural Science:* Can human consciousness and rationality be explained completely in evolutionary terms? Concerning the origins of the universe, can science explain the Big Bang, or does this event point beyond itself to causes outside the bounds of science?

> *Political Science:* Is representative democracy the most "Christian" form of government possible? If so, then how

far should one go to create such a system in non-democratic nations? Is a "war for democracy" worth the cost?

Economics: Is a tax system that takes money from the wealthy to distribute to the poor a proper application of biblical social ethics, or is it an infringement on the Christian notion of human freedom? Should governments regulate the economy merely to ensure a level playing field, or to achieve greater economic equality?

Literature: To what extent are we obligated to read a text according to the author's original purpose? Is it possible to transcend the bounds of race, class, gender, and culture and truly understand an author's intent? In other words, is there anything truly universal in Shakespeare?

Music and Art: Is beauty simply in the eye of the beholder, or are there external, objective standards of beauty that can be applied to all works of art? Does the eight-note major scale sound "right" to us simply because we have been conditioned that way, or because it corresponds to some universal standard created by God? Are some art forms more "Christian" than others?

Questions such as these abound in every discipline, and their value is that they challenge us not only to know our discipline, but to think more deeply about our Christian faith and its implications for the world around us.

Integrative questions also lead to another observation: The integration of faith and learning continues throughout one's life as a Christian learner. One does not "get" integration in an introductory college class and then go on to other topics in one's subject. Remember the crossword puzzle metaphor in the opening chapter? Because our Christian worldview is dynamic, not static, integration is a two-way street. That is, our Christian worldview affects the subject we study, but the truth learned in that subject may in turn influence our Christian worldview. This back-and-forth process continues throughout our lives as Christian learners.

Here's an example in history: As a Christian historian, I have been interested in the study of American slavery, and my Christian worldview affects my understanding of the topic in a variety of ways: The lives of seemingly insignificant individual slaves are worth studying because they are human beings made in God's image; as a historian I can to some extent understand the causes and course of slavery in history because God has ordered the universe in a rational, cause-and-effect manner; one should expect to find evidence that religion played an important role in the slaves' lives because as creatures made in God's image human beings are inherently religious. These are all assumptions that I bring to my study of slavery because of my Christian faith.

> *Our Christian worldview affects the subject we study, but the truth learned in that subject may in turn influence our Christian worldview. This back-and-forth process continues throughout our lives as Christian learners.*

My study of slavery, however, also impacts my Christian worldview. For example, many of the slaves were devout Christians. Thus, one thing that the history of slavery reveals is that God sometimes allows his people to spend their lives in seemingly meaningless, unfulfilling occupations such as picking cotton. Such a conclusion challenges my modern American middle-class assumption that the Christian who is "in God's will" should automatically be engaged in a fulfilling career. Also, this basic fact—that the slave communities were generally Christian—leads me to question the conventional Christian belief that America has represented "God's Country" throughout much of its history. In fact, the study of slavery suggests that nineteenth-century America may have more closely resembled a "New Egypt," enslaving God's chosen people, than it did a "New Israel." It may motivate me as a Christian to better appreciate the racial conflict that has existed in American history and work to promote racial reconciliation. As the study of history demonstrates, this dialectical process of adjustment and re-adjustment between our Christian worldview and what we learn continues throughout our lives. Integration, therefore, is a permanent part of a healthy Christian life.

In closing, let me offer a word of caution: Consciously integrating faith and learning by asking the "big questions" will not always comprise the majority of a course at the Christian college, nor should it. As Christians, we can and should ask the big questions of all subjects, but much of our time will be spent on the more mundane level of doing basic scholarship in the discipline. Looking back on my college basketball days, my most vivid memories are playing intense games against rival teams, especially those games in the national tournament. But measured in terms of time, those partic-ular experiences were not the norm. As any athlete knows, most of my actual time playing basketball was spent doing drills, practicing plays, working on fundamentals, and worst of all, running sprints. The countless hours engaged in such activities provided the foun-dation for those games that I remember so vividly.

The application to academics is obvious. Asking the big ques-tions in a particular discipline is only possible if one understands the subject in the first place. A class on trigonometry will not get very far if students constantly interrupt the professor to ask, "Are logarithms discovered or invented?" While such questions are important, they should not prevent us from doing the hard work of understand-ing the details of the subject itself. It does one little good to debate the significance of cell structures to the theory of evolution if one doesn't understand how mitochondria function in the first place. In other words, integrating faith and learning in biology is not an al-ternative to the important task of memorizing the stages of mitosis.

Hence, the calling of the Christian in college is not very differ-ent from the Christian life in general. Our big tasks as Christians such as redeeming creation and making disciples usually manifest themselves in simple faithfulness to seemingly mundane tasks like showing up for work on time and helping one's neighbor. In the same way, the lofty calling of a Christian college student—understanding God's creation and becoming an agent of redemption in the world—generally works itself out in simple ways such as going to class and faithfully pursuing one's calling as a Christian learner.

A Note on Sources

The integration of faith and learning has become a widely-discussed subject at Christian colleges and among Christian scholars. Thus, books and articles on the subject abound—one bibliography on the subject lists 348 volumes. For this brief introduction, I have drawn from several sources, most notably Arthur Holmes's *The Idea of a Christian College* (Eerdmans, 1996). The discussion of the Implicit/Explicit Continuum is drawn from C. Stephen Evans, "The Calling of the Christian Scholar-Teacher," in Douglas Henry and Bob Agee, eds., *Faithful Learning and the Christian Scholarly Vocation* (Eerdmans, 2003), 26-49, and from Douglas and Rhonda Jacobsen, eds., *Scholarship and Christian Faith: Enlarging the Conversation* (Oxford University Press, 2004). Heie's notion of the integrative question can be found in Harry Lee Poe's *Christianity in the Academy* (Baker Academic, 2004), 158-160.

Questions for Reflection and Discussion

1. Have you encountered any of these mistaken views of integration in your academic career?

2. Why do some subjects lend themselves to integration more explicitly than other subjects?

3. What would be an example of an "integrative question" in your major field of study?

4. Why would a course at a Christian college not necessarily spend most of its time consciously integrating faith and learning?

5. Do you think it would be better to emphasize the integration of faith and learning in a freshman-level course or in a senior-level course? Explain.

7 AN EDUCATION THAT LASTS

Thinking Creatively and Globally

IMAGINE the following scenario: You aspire to compete in the Olympics someday. You arrange your lifestyle so that you can become a world-class athlete—you get plenty of sleep, carefully monitor your diet, and of course spend hours a day in training and preparation. But here's the catch: The Olympic organizers have decided that it would be fun to change the Olympic events every four years, and to keep the events secret until a week before the games begin. How would you prepare for the Olympics? Naturally, you would focus on activities that make you as flexible and adaptable as possible. Weight-training would be crucial; but you would not want to bulk up like a Russian weight-lifter because you might be called upon to run the hundred-meter dash. It would be important to develop your hand-eye coordination for table tennis, but also hone your footwork in case you are called upon to do the triple jump.

While such a scenario may be far-fetched in athletics, it's not very far from the world that today's college students enter upon graduation. As Thomas Friedman, author of *The World Is Flat*, notes, in today's globalized, decentralized, and rapidly-changing world, preparing for the future is like "training for the Olympics without knowing which sport you will compete in." What kind of college education best prepares students for such a world? Actually, it's the very education that most Christian colleges provide: a liberal arts-based, globally oriented education.

That last sentence will need some unpacking. The previous chapters have focused on the *Christian* dimensions of education by explaining a Christian worldview and the integration of faith and learning. But most Christian colleges also describe their educational program as including the liberal arts. Unfortunately, while educators like to throw the "liberal arts" phrase around, few people outside of academia know what the term means or why it is used. This concluding chapter, therefore, will explore the nature of a liberal arts education and explain why such an education is so valuable in today's society.

The liberal arts as an educational program emerged about 2,500 years ago in ancient Greece. In democratic Athens, the free citizen needed to be able to speak persuasively and eloquently in a public forum. Thus a "liberal arts" education in the classical world focused on grammar—for the study of texts—and "rhetoric" or the art of persuasive speech. With the rise of Christianity in the late Roman Empire, the liberal arts became grafted onto the needs of Christian education, namely biblical interpretation, the study of theology, and the nurture of personal piety. Medieval Christian universities expanded the subjects of the liberal arts to include not only grammar, rhetoric, and logic but also math, music, and astronomy.

During the Protestant Reformation of the 1500s, Reformers such as Martin Luther and John Calvin developed a system of education that combined Christian instruction and classical learning. It was designed to produce what they called a "wise and eloquent piety." As we have seen, such a curriculum became the norm at early American colleges such as Harvard and Yale. The rise of modern science to pre-eminence in the 1800s, however, challenged this traditional liberal arts program, and universities changed in two ways. First, the liberal arts were expanded to include natural and social sciences such as biology and psychology. Second, colleges allowed students to select a particular "major" or course of study that would prepare them for a specific career. In most cases, however, specialized majors did not simply replace the liberal arts. Rather, the two curricula were combined into a four-year undergraduate program.

> *A liberal arts course seeks to connect the non-specialist to a historical conversation about some of the big questions in life that have been on-going within a particular discipline.*

Thus, most Christian colleges today combine study in a major with a liberal arts core, which they call "general education" or "core curriculum." So what makes something a "core" class? First, a liberal arts course seeks to connect the non-specialist to a historical conversation about some of the big questions in life that have been on-going within a particular discipline. For example, a core class in introductory biology will not only cover the five phases of mitosis but also explore the big questions in the discipline such as, "What is life? Where did it come from? What is unique about humans?" And of course, at a Christian college such a course will challenge students to integrate a Christian worldview with such questions. To put it in the terms of the previous chapter, a Christian core class will deal with integrative questions, not just technical questions.

Second, a liberal arts course primarily seeks to impact who we *are* rather than what we do. It develops internal qualities such as depth of insight, clarity of understanding, appreciation for cultural activity, communication skill, and moral commitment. Once again, an analogy from sports may be helpful. As a basketball player, I can benefit both from practicing my free throw technique and from lifting weights. Practicing free throws improves a particular skill that I need in a basketball game. Weight training benefits me indirectly in basketball, but also in other sports as well. We can think of major courses as free throw training, providing specific knowledge or skills that are needed for a particular "game." Core classes, by contrast, are more like weight training. They develop who we are at a more fundamental level. Thus, they prepare us for a wider variety of activities, but their practical value may be more obscure than a specific course in a major.

So why are the liberal arts still important today? To answer that question, let's look more closely at the world that today's college graduates will enter. Two recent books describe that world and have tremendous implications for college education today. The first is Daniel Pink's *A Whole New Mind: Why Right-Brainers Will Rule the Future* (Penguin, 2005). Pink tells the story of the past two centuries with a broad but fairly accurate brush. The nineteenth century, he explains, was known as the Industrial Age. New machines were invented that replaced human physical power and produced goods more efficiently than ever before. The changes deeply affected Western society as factories emerged, populations shifted from the farm to the city, and economies increased in complexity. As a result, universities expanded to educate citizens to function more effectively in an industrial society.

In the twentieth century the modern western nations entered a new phase, the Information Age, in which knowledge and information fed the economies of advanced nations. Professions developed, and a new social class came to dominate society, the "white collar" class. The most advanced societies consisted of "knowledge workers" who produced and processed information. For example, factories that produced automobiles could be moved to Mexico where industrial workers were cheaper, but the managers needed to plan, develop, and distribute the cars remained in their offices in Detroit. In such a world, the desirable traits of college graduates were "left-brained" traits such as linear thinking and logical analysis. Law, computer programming, and engineering were the seemingly safe professions that would always provide job security and a good paycheck.

The twenty-first century, however, has witnessed yet another transformation. Advanced societies have reached a level of affluence in which design and aesthetics, not just utility, are desirable traits. In a world of economic choices, consumers want automobiles that are not only practical but aesthetically pleasing. Products that "feel" right, such as the iPad, win out over those that do not. Furthermore, advances in technology and communications, most notably the internet, mean that even complex tasks can be automated and outsourced to other locations. Twenty years ago you would have paid an accountant to prepare your taxes. Now you can purchase and download TurboTax to perform the same function. In the Information Age, a law degree seemingly guaranteed the graduate lifetime job security and a good income. Today, however, the internet is breaking through the information monopoly that has long been the source of security to lawyers. Need a divorce? CompleteCase.com will handle it for a mere $249. In other words, just as machines replaced human power to dig coal shafts in the 1800s, new technologies and global communications today are demonstrating the ability to replace the knowledge workers of the twentieth century.

Thus, we have entered what Pink calls the Conceptual Age, one in which creators, designers, and collaborators command the highest value. The right brain—the part that synthesizes information, sees the big picture, envisions new scenarios, and empathizes with others—is as essential to the modern economy as the left brain. Any computer programmer can write code for an iPhone. But it takes a different sort of mind to envision the need and value of an iPhone in the first place, and to design one that has that mysterious quality of "feeling right" to the user. In other words, *creativity*, not computation, is the important trait of the future.

There's another important change in the modern world. The programmer writing code for the iPhone—or fielding your phone call when your computer screen freezes up—is more likely to be sitting in a converted warehouse in Mumbai, India, than in Silicon Valley. Such a fact points to another fundamental transformation described by Thomas Friedman in *The World Is Flat: A Brief History of the Twenty-First Century* (Farrar, 2005). Advances in technology and communications have produced a "flat," rapidly-changing world in which goods are produced through global supply chains and workers in America compete with workers in Brazil and China. The typical corporation today is multi-national. The concept for a car may originate in Detroit, but the design plans may be developed in Germany, the parts produced in Mexico, and the car assembled in Alabama. Furthermore, the rise of the internet means that the free market can pinpoint the cheapest labor source, whether that is in sewing garments or writing computer code. In other words, "outsourcing" affects not just factory workers but computer programmers.

A technological, rapidly-changing global economy means that nations at the cutting edge of these changes such as the United States will increasingly find their niche in the "soft" areas described by Daniel Pink. Creative work will occupy a growing segment of the American economy. Of course, we still need people to grow food and build houses. But college graduates in America will be expected to do the creative work of research and development, designing new products, and collaborating with workers in other cultures. The modern situation is depicted in the following graphic from the National Center on Education and the Economy:

Prototypical U.S. Industry in Ten Years

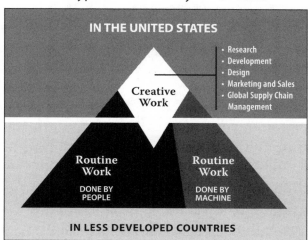

All of this naturally has tremendous implications for colleges in the United States. Education for a "flat" world, Friedman notes, must focus on "teaching students how to learn, instilling passion and curiosity in them, and developing their intuitive skills." A generation ago many Americans saw the value of a college education as primarily training a graduate in specific job skills. Today a college education has to prepare graduates to think creatively, work effectively with people from diverse cultures, and adapt quickly to technological and social changes. To return to our Olympics analogy—if Americans a generation ago went to college to prepare to be pole vaulters, students today must prepare to be decathletes.

So what does this all mean for the college freshman who just wants to get a college degree and not have to worry about computer programmers in Mumbai? Specifically, such a social transformation has three lessons for the Christian college student:

1. Don't stress out over a major.

In a world where technologies change rapidly and whole new economies can emerge on short notice, the particular major that one pursues in college is less important than the overall qualities, knowledge base, and skills that one develops. A few years ago, *USA Today* surveyed the undergraduate majors of Chief Executive Offices of Fortune 500 companies. Surprisingly, only fifteen percent of them had majored in business, and a large number of them majored in seemingly esoteric liberal arts disciplines such as philosophy, art history, or literature. In light of the social changes discussed above, such a fact should not be surprising. A major such as philosophy develops the sort of critical reasoning and communication skills that one would expect from a leader of a modern corporation.

To alleviate "major stress" among my college freshmen, I used to play a match game in which students attempt to match university officials with their major in college. To their surprise, students discovered that their college president was an English major, the vice president for student development was a psychology major, and the chief financial officer majored in, of all things, zoology. Of course, the student who wants to be an engineer will have to get started on an engineering degree right away. But for the vast majority of college students, the fluid, global work environment means that what one majors in is much less important than the broader skills and perspectives that a college education will provide. As one business executive remarked, "Everybody ten years out of college is doing something completely different from what they went to college for and majored in."

For the vast majority of college students, the fluid, global work environment means that what one majors in is much less important than the broader skills and perspectives that a college education will provide.

Moreover, the skills that one develops in supposedly impractical majors may bear fruit in unexpected ways, as my own career demonstrates. I majored in history, mainly because I had no idea what I wanted to do in life and I liked reading stories about the past. In some ways, my history major directly impacted my career since I went on to complete a Ph.D. in history and become a professor. But now I am an academic administrator, and the history volumes collecting dust on my bookshelves primarily serve to lend a nice scholarly atmosphere to my office. So was my history major irrelevant to my current career as an administrator? Certainly not. The primary skill that I learned as a historian was to wade through a mountain of historical facts, perceive the big picture amid the details, and create a reasonable, compelling story out of the data. The infinite number of events that occurred in eastern North America in the 1770s and 1780s, for example, don't simply explain themselves. It takes a historian to select events, find a common thread, and tell the story of the American Revolution from such events.

I no longer write history books, but I do interpret data. For example, one of my responsibilities is to prepare updates on academics twice a year for the Board of Trustees. I have a wealth of data at my disposal: student graduation rates, course evaluations, enrollment data by major, curricular changes, faculty professional activities, etc. But trustees do not want a pile of data; they want a *story* that explains what the current academic situation is and where it is going. My job is to sift through the facts, perceive the story that the data is telling, and communicate that story in a compelling way to the trustees. In other words, I am an administrator but I am functioning as a historian. Twenty years ago when I wrote a paper on Japan during World War II, I had no idea that I would be using the same skills someday to write a trustee report as an administrator.

The lesson is clear: Because we cannot predict how society will change, much less our own careers, the choice of a particular major is less important than the transferable skills that one learns both in a major and in other courses. Some students spend too much time worrying about choosing a major instead of focusing on the overall learning that they gain in college. Which leads to the second lesson:

2. Take the liberal arts core seriously.

One sometimes hears students refer to core curriculum courses as stuff to "get out of the way" so that they can focus on the more important courses in their major. Interestingly enough, however, that's not the kind of rhetoric one hears from employers. A recent survey of business executives in America revealed that 67% of them preferred college graduates who either had a well-rounded education focusing on broad knowledge and skills, or an undergraduate program that combined broad knowledge with training in a specific field. Only 22% endorsed an undergraduate program that focused solely on education in a specific field. As one executive remarked, "I look for people who take accountability, responsibility, and are good team people over anything else. I can teach the technical."

The features of a global and creative world should make it clear how short-sighted "getting general education out of the way" is, and why employers want graduates with a balanced education. The liberal arts are designed to nurture the very qualities of mind that are most essential in a global age. For example, the study of literature develops an awareness of narrative, the ability to read critically and insightfully, and the ability to see the world from

> *The liberal arts are designed to nurture the very qualities of mind most needed in a global age.*

another perspective. The study of politics develops a sense of power structures, group interactions, and an awareness of how institutions function that may become valuable in a corporate job someday.

This is not to say you should become an art history major if you want to be CEO of Microsoft—nor that you should drop out of college altogether as Bill Gates did. But even students who major in highly-specialized disciplines such as engineering need to take the liberal arts seriously. That point was made clear recently in "Holistic Engineering," an insightful article by Domenico Grasso, dean of the College of Engineering at the University of Vermont, and David Martinelli, chair of the department of engineering at West Virginia University. Because technology is becoming ever more complex and "increasingly embedded in the human experience," they observe, engineers need to think beyond the narrow bounds of their discipline. "A new kind of engineer is needed," they write, "one who can think broadly across disciplines and consider the human dimensions that are at the heart of every design challenge."

Grasso and Martinelli argue that engineers must think holistically for both moral and practical reasons. First, engineering is a discipline that purports to design for humanity and improve the quality of human life. To do so, engineers must attempt "to understand the human condition in all its complexity—which requires the study of literature, history, philosophy, religion, and economics." Furthermore, in a "flat" world where applied technology can be outsourced to Asia, they argue, American engineers need to find their niche as innovative problem *definers*, not just technical problem solvers. Their conclusion: Engineers today must be trained not only in their field but need to develop the ability to think "powerfully and critically in many other disciplines." Of course, that is exactly what a liberal arts core is designed to teach.

If in today's economy even engineers need a broad liberal arts education, the same is certainly true of lawyers, economists, teachers, and graphic designers. The liberal arts are not something to get out of the way but are essential to an effective undergraduate education.

3. Go global.

In today's increasingly flat world, one trait that ranks high on the list of desirable qualities is the ability to understand and collaborate with people from different cultures. Even college graduates who never plan to venture outside of the U.S. will have to function cross-culturally in the American economy. Given current demographic trends, the U.S. Census Bureau predicts that the United States will be a "minority culture" by the year 2042. That is, in a few decades no single ethnic group will comprise a majority of the population, as Caucasians currently do. Moreover, the ability to function cross-culturally is not something that one learns by sitting in a classroom and reading a book about a different culture. You have to get out there and experience the culture. That's why a cross-cultural study program is one of the most valuable experiences that students report when they graduate. Eighty-three percent of college graduates who studied abroad during their undergraduate years rated the experience as having a significant impact on their lives, higher than their responses for both college friendships and classroom work.

The most valuable undergraduate education, therefore, includes some significant time of study in another culture. There is simply no substitute for the experience of getting on an airplane and landing in a world where the signs are unreadable, the food is strange, and you are challenged to understand and communicate with people who see the world differently than you do. Cross-cultural study provides an incredible opportunity to learn new things, but it also provides a mirror on your culture and prods you to question your own beliefs and perspective. Indeed, foreign travel is one of the best ways that we learn to adjust and broaden our own Christian worldview. As G. K. Chesterton once remarked, the purpose of travel is not simply to set foot on foreign land. "It is at last to set foot on one's *own* country as a foreign land." That's what an undergraduate education is all about.

> *There is simply no substitute for the experience of getting in an airplane and landing in a world where the signs are unreadable, the food is strange, and you are challenged to understand and communicate with people who see the world differently than you do.*

Because it takes time to learn a new culture, the ideal cross-cultural experience is a full semester studying abroad. And most Christian colleges today provide ample opportunities to spend a semester studying in China, Europe, or other parts of the world. Many students, however, cannot spend an entire semester away from their home university. Fortunately, research indicates that in some ways, at least, even a short term abroad has as much impact on students as a full semester. A recent survey of college graduates indicated that students who studied abroad for four weeks or less were just as likely to be globally engaged as students who spent a semester abroad. Moreover, short-term study abroad programs abound at Christian colleges, either during the summer months, in a January term, or both. Students who want to get the most out of their undergraduate education will take the opportunity to experience another culture through a study abroad trip.

In sum, an education that lasts well beyond your college years is one that prepares you not only to think holistically and creatively, but that enables you to think globally and function cross-culturally. "The world is a book," Augustine said, "and those who do not travel read only a page."

All of this discussion of the practical benefits of a liberal arts education may seem inconsistent with the previous chapters' discussion of the Christian foundations of education. But there's no reason why a Christian liberal arts education cannot be both good for its own sake but also make sense practically. When I was a child, Campbell's soup ran a marketing campaign designed to appeal both to children and their parents. "Campbell's soup is not just good," the slogan went. "It's good *for* you." We can think of a Christian liberal arts education in the same way. Because of the doctrine of creation, learning is intrinsically good. God created the world, and he created humans in his own image to understand his creation, to delight in it, and to develop it in new and creative ways. Education is also good because as God's people in a fallen world, we become more effective co-redeemers with God when we have the skills and insights that a college education provides.

But being intrinsically good doesn't mean that a college education cannot also be good *for* you. Because God is the creator of all things, at some level "good" and "good for you" become virtually inseparable. Physical health, for example, is good for its own sake; but in general, a healthy person is also able to accomplish more in life than an unhealthy person. Similarly, the intrinsically good insights and skills that we acquire as God's image-bearers also prepare us to function effectively in a global economy where creativity, critical thinking, teamwork, and effective communication are vital qualities. A robust, globally focused Christian education centered on the liberal arts is truly good *and* good for you.

A Note on Sources

Thomas Friedman's comments on higher education are found in Jeffrey Selingo, "Rethinking Higher Education for a Changing World," *Chronicle of Higher Education* (July 12, 2006). The history of the liberal arts is found in Cornelius Plantinga's *Engaging God's World* (Eerdmans, 2002), 191-197. The graphic "The Prototypical U.S. Industry in Ten Years" is found in the Executive Summary of "Tough Choices or Tough Times," a report by the National Center on Education and the Economy, 2007. The survey of Fortune 500 CEOs was published in *USA Today's* "Offbeat Majors Help CEOs Think Outside the Box," (July 24, 2001). The survey of business executives is in "How Should Colleges Prepare Students to Succeed in Today's Global Economy?" by Peter D. Hart Research Associates, Inc., 2006. Grasso and Martinelli's "Holistic Engineering" was published in the *Chronicle of Higher Education* (March 16, 2007). The survey of study abroad students is found in Karin Fischer, "Short Study-Abroad Trips," *Chronicle of Higher Education* (February 20, 2009). G. K. Chesterton's quote is from his work *Tremendous Trifles* (Dodd and Mead, 1920), 245-246.

Questions for Reflection and Discussion

1. Should Christian colleges prescribe a set list of required "core" classes, or give students flexibility to choose their own courses? Explain.

2. What liberal arts courses, if any, do you think should be required by a Christian college? Why?

3. What would the notion of "creativity, not computation" look like in your field of study or intended career?

4. Why would a person need to learn to think holistically in a field such as Business or Education? Give a specific example.

5. Why is cross-cultural study important in today's world? What sort of experience or program would relate best to your interests or major?